"With *Dealing With Difficult Passages*, Dr. Maslin has boldly waded into waters where angels fear to tread. The book covers a wide range of topics and lives up to its title. It is an excellent tool for teachers, students and all who desire to grapple with tough passages we have all pondered. Not all will agree with his conclusions but his work will make you come to grips with your own understanding of these issues. It's worth your read any way you measure it. The author has done his homework and it may lead you to do yours."

Jim Henry
Pastor First Baptist Church, Orlando, Florida, 1977-2006
President of the Southern Baptist Convention, 1994-1996

"Dr. Roger Maslin is well-qualified to write about dealing with difficult passages and doctrines of the Scriptures. With years of pastoral experience and strong Biblical knowledge, he adequately speaks to these difficulties. I have praised God for his effective ministry. You will be blessed as God speaks to you through Dr. Maslin's written work."

Dr. Bill W. Coffman
Former President, Florida Baptist Convention
Former foreign missionary, Southern Baptist Convention
Former Director, Language Missions, Florida Baptist Convention
Pastor of local churches for 58 years

"It is difficult to commend to others Dr. Roger Maslin's masterful book, *Dealing with Difficulties*, in only a few words or sentences. The reason is because he deals with such an expansive number of issues that have been the source of controversy and misunderstanding for pastors and laypersons through the years. Suffice it to say that Dr. Maslin's examination of each of the difficult issues he raises in his book demonstrates clarity, consistency, conciseness and conviction. And, most of all, his conclusions are overwhelmingly compelling. Every pastor or teacher needs to read this book."

Dr. Ken Mahanes
Special Advisor to the President
Palm Beach Atlantic University

DEALING WITH THE DIFFICULT

Examining Biblical Beliefs

DR. ROGER W. MASLIN

WESTBOW
PRESS®
A DIVISION OF THOMAS NELSON
& ZONDERVAN

Scripture taken from the King James Version of the Bible.
Scripture taken from the ASV American Standard Version.
Scripture taken from the CEV Contemporary English Version.
Scripture taken from the HCSB Holcomb Christian Standard Bible.
Scripture taken from the ISV International Standard Version.
Scripture taken from the LITV Literal Translation of the Holy Bible
Scripture taken from the RV Revised Version
Scripture taken from the YLT Young's Literal Translation

Scripture quotations are from The Holy Bible, English Standard Version® (ESV®), copyright © 2001 by Crossway, a publishing ministry of Good News Publishers. Used by permission. All rights reserved.

All Scripture quotations in this publications are from The Message. Copyright (c) by Eugene H. Peterson 1993, 1994, 1995, 1996, 2000, 2001, 2002. Used by permission of NavPress Publishing Group.

Scripture quotations taken from the Holy Bible, New Living Translation, copyright 1996, 2004. Used by permission of Tyndale House Publishers, Inc., Wheaton, Illinois 60189. All rights reserved.

WestBow Press books may be ordered through booksellers or by contacting:

WestBow Press
A Division of Thomas Nelson & Zondervan
1663 Liberty Drive
Bloomington, IN 47403
www.westbowpress.com
1 (866) 928-1240

ISBN: 978-1-5127-0423-5 (sc)
ISBN: 978-1-5127-0425-9 (hc)
ISBN: 978-1-5127-0424-2 (e)

Print information available on the last page.

WestBow Press rev. date: 11/09/2015

C O N T E N T S

PART III DIFFICULT ESCHATOLOGY (END TIME EVENTS)

IN HONOR OF

My Daughter Cindy,

Faithful Servant of Christ,

Encourager, Assistant and Efficient Manager

INTRODUCTION

This is not a book about dealing with difficult people, for there are many with their various personality traits. That would be a challenge. Many of them could be helped with loving counsel and discipline, but that is not my area of expertise. There are many that have written extensively in this area of concern. As I write <u>Dealing With the Difficult</u>, I am dealing with difficult Bible passages, doctrines and difficult eschatology.

This is not a book dealing with some of the great and dreaded experiences of life, such as sickness, disease, death, sorrow and grief. Every Christian can contribute to the expertise of those well trained to deal with these experiences as we practice the ministry of comfort and understanding. We can respect the work of others, and we can also understand these experiences from what God has revealed in His Word. And we do sorrow, but not like those who have no hope.

Dealing with the difficult is not about dealing with the impossible. It is about facing the difficult, and seeking a reasonable, sensible, solution. It is a difficult process because the tendency in all of us is to look for an easy way out. That search ignores the possibilities, glosses over any attempt to solve the contradictions, and promotes shallow thinking. In examining the professed beliefs of Christians, we will not avoid the controversial. That is not the path to truth. Conflicting opinions are only evidence that the arguments need to be closely examined.

My interest in writing this book has to do with difficult passages in the scriptures, difficult doctrines where there is not always agreement, and difficult eschatology where many entertain different positions on end time events. It is amazing how many seem to know so much that just isn't true.

To acquire sound doctrine from the Word of God ought to be the goal of every Christian. It should never be despaired. To revise or discard previously held beliefs, in many cases, is more difficult and painful, than to learn correctly from the start. This may occur for various reasons. We may have been taught wrong and did not have all of the available facts. We all experience this process at different times in our lives for all of the previous mentioned reasons. But if we stop learning and think we know it all, then nothing seems to change. This is an unnecessary path to ignorance. I have even seen in my own ministry many Christians who feel they have learned everything they need to know about the Christian life and the Scriptures from listening to one pastor.

The disciples of our Lord often misunderstood the nature of His kingdom. They did not grasp the spiritual nature of the kingdom. Paul, steeped in Judaism, misunderstood God's special love for all believers, regardless of race or ethnicity. His conversion on the road to Damascus changed that with his regeneration experience. The disciples misunderstood God's love for the Gentiles and God made it plain to them at the house of Cornelius. The bewitched Galatian Christians evidently had not grasped the purity, finality and nature of the Gospel message. So they were susceptible to introducing Judaism into it. Paul had to set them straight. He had to even oppose Peter to his face to correct the misunderstanding being perpetuated in their midst. It is in the area of eschatology that I have had to unlearn the most.

So the burden of my message is to rightly divide the word of truth, to explain the difficult, and perhaps to help some revise and correct a few of their strongly held opinions. I believe that this will occur when dealing with difficult doctrines. I also believe that every lover of the

Lord and His Word should be open to new truths. That is a part of growing in grace and knowledge.

I have found the Internet program, **E-Sword**, is a great tool for Bible Study. It includes some of the most popular versions of the Bible as well as the classical commentaries. I refer to them often in this study book. I appreciate their aid to understanding. It encourages me to further study. At the same time, I am also prone to criticize their writings because I feel they are too wordy. That was acceptable in their time and has provided a foundation for the newer writers to pursue conciseness. People today require conciseness. It is difficult in itself to understand the commentaries as to their message. I hope that I can avoid vagueness and be as "clear as a bell" to enhance understanding. I will not avoid controversy because to do so would only add further confusion. I do not ever want to conclude: "I don't know what to believe."

Abbreviations for these Commentaries are: MH=Matthew Henry; JFB=Jamieson, Fausset, and Brown; GILL=John Gill. I also use different versions of the Bible to make clearer the message I am tying to convey. They are the KJV for the authorized version, which is my favorite; The Revised Standard Version (RSV); The American Standard Version (ASV); The Contemporary English Version (CEV); The English Standard Version (ESV); and the Literal Translation of the Bible (LITTV).

PART I

DIFFICULT PASSAGES

CHAPTER 1

Falling Away in the Book of Hebrews

There are two passages in the book of Hebrews that mention an experience of "falling away" or "drawing back." We want to look at them carefully to determine what they teach and what they do not teach.

Hebrews 6:4-8: For it is impossible to keep on restoring to repentance time and again people who have once been enlightened, who have tasted the heavenly gift, who have become sharers of the Holy Spirit, who have tasted the goodness of God's word and the powers of the coming age, and who have fallen away, as long as they continue to crucify to themselves the Son of God and to expose him to public ridicule. (*International Standard Version*, hereafter as ISV)

Hebrews 10:38, 39: But my righteous one will live by faith, and if he turns back, my soul will take no pleasure in him. Now, we do not belong to those who turn back and are destroyed, but to those who have faith and are saved. (ISV)

WHAT THESE SCRIPTURES DO NOT TEACH

Some have resorted to these verses as proof texts that a saved person can be lost. Even though we may have different interpretations of what they do mean, it is clear from other Scriptures that the security of the believer should not be questioned. There is not even a hint that a born again person can be unborn and forever lost. Those who believe that you can lose your salvation by committing one sin, or many sins, can really find no comfort in these passages of Scripture. For one thing, the passage describes the persons as being "impossible to renew to repentance." Furthermore, the inspired writer makes it plain, "Beloved, we are persuaded better things of you, and things that accompany salvation." (Hebrews 6:9) And in Hebrews 10:39, he assures the believers: "But we are not of them that draw back unto perdition; but of them that believe to the saving of the soul."

We could best learn what these Scriptures do not teach, before proceeding to the positive teaching. We want to avoid any error in making the right interpretation. We can safely affirm that no person, who by the regenerative act of God, having been created a new person in Christ, can have that new birth reversed. A powerful and unanswerable reason is, because that new person is said to be "in Christ." That being true, the believer is also in the Father's hand, and nobody can take the believer out of the Father's hand, because He is greater than all the powers of hell, manifested in the work of the devil. The devil and demons cannot accomplish that task, and nothing is able to separate us from God's love, because it is eternal.

It is also true that the believer in Christ cannot apostatize and lose his salvation. Can that one backslide? Absolutely! We all backslide. It is just a matter of degree, not if. We all yield to temptation, because we still have the old nature in us that wars against the new nature.

We do not claim to be perfect. If we claim that we have never sinned, we only deceive ourselves. The truth is not in us. In other words, we are liars. That is a strong accusation, but it is true. I have heard of other people who claim to have never sinned since they were saved. They must have received a different new nature than I did. God has declared clearly that "all have sinned;" nowhere does He claim that we shall be free from future sin. We all face the possibility of strong temptation, and must prayerfully guard against it. Yielding to that kind of testing is universal. Repentance, confession and receiving the gift of forgiveness is the solution when we fail.

A HELPFUL GLOSSARY

Often the author of a book will give you a list of technical, foreign, or uncommon words with a brief definition. There are many words or phrases in these two passages in Hebrews where that is needed. In this case, we have to go to different translations, and commentaries, or the original Greek, to make our identifications.

Enlightened "here means *knowledge of the word of truth."* (Jamieson, Fausset, Brown, hereafter as JFB) **Who have tasted of the heavenly gift** — These words connote a sense of light, followed by taste, as figures for the act of appropriating the heavenly gift of forgiveness. We are enlightened by the preached Word. We follow by accepting the message, deciding to follow Christ. That's tasting. The writer uses another phrase to describe the same experience which is to be made **partakers of the Holy Ghost.** This phrase includes the work of the Holy Spirit. It is distinguished from, but is inseparably connected with, "enlightened," and "tasted of the heavenly gift." It may be described as being a partner of the Holy Spirit. **Crucify to themselves the Son of God afresh** — these are simply identifying them selves with the crucifiers of Christ, and He cannot be crucified again. His crucifixion was for our sins, and it was one exclusive, sufficient, eternal sacrifice for our sins which can never be repeated, and for which there is no need.

The world to come looked forward to all that would be happening in the age of grace. The grace has already begun and we are yet to witness its future glories. **Fall away** is deviating from the true way and following a false, destructive way. It may be described as standing off from the Saviour, or just falling aside. Both have the same result. They put the Saviour **"to an open shame"** which treats Him as a deserving malefactor exposed to public ridicule, treating Him as one on display. Those are pretty strong words to describe their sin. **Perdition** is a word used to describe the ultimate destination of such persons so described. Turning back they are destroyed, forever damned. **Apostasy** is the abandonment of faith, the tenets of the Christian faith which they have understood and previously embraced.

EXPLANATIONS OFFERED

Now that we are assured that real believers do not "fall away," or "draw back unto perdition," we look for better explanations. They cannot all be right and some may be better than others, but what we are looking for is an explanation (1) that does not contradict other Scriptures, and (2) is loyal to the overall message of the author.

1. The unsaved explanation. Those who accept this explanation hold that the passage refers to those who have professed to experience redemption and accept the knowledge of the truth. They have come close to making a genuine decision, but never followed through to salvation. So there would never be a chance for them to be redeemed. If they reject the grace way of salvation, there is not, and never will be, another way for those individuals to be redeemed.

2. The apostasy explanation. Briefly stated, this is the view that believes the writer to the Hebrews is explaining how far a person can go in the Christian life and turn back, turn away, or fall away totally. This apostasy is final, and it would be impossible to "renew them again unto repentance." Evidently, that is the position of many in interpreting these

verses. Apostasy is real, and this is a pretty good definition of apostasy; but if the reference is to an experience of believers, the explanation does not fit because true believers cannot apostatize. John Wesley also calls them "willful total apostates." This might be the easiest explanation of these verses - but is it the correct one?

3. The hypothetical explanation. The author is presenting a hypothetical case which amounts to the fact that the Hebrew Christians are in danger of apostatizing from Jesus. How could this even be possible? It couldn't, as attested by the bulk of Scriptures that indicate that it is impossible for the true believer to apostatize. The situation could not possibly be real, because the writer is "persuaded better things" of them. To me, this seems like a pretty flimsy explanation.

4. The persevering explanation. Another explanation is the claim that the author has in mind a persevering faith. The only persevering faith is a saving faith. Those who endure to the end shall be saved. On this, both Arminians and Calvinists seem to agree. But they are incompatible in their beliefs, since the former believe a person can be lost after they have been saved and be saved all over again, while the latter hold to the eternal security of the believer. So they differ on the definition of persevering faith. The Arminian view mixes works with persevering faith, as though a person can and must keep his own salvation by his own efforts. That in itself is impossible. No person can effect salvation, nor can he keep it. It is a work of God in regenerating the lost man. Thus, the whole Arminian scheme falls apart, since this Scripture affirms that it is impossible to renew them to repentance and faith.

5. The arrested spiritual development explanation. This is the explanation of Hobbs, and I believe the evidence supports it. He believes that the author is speaking of the born again person. They are not in danger of apostatizing and losing their salvation, but they have a problem with arrested spiritual growth. They are stagnant in the Christian life. They are standing still rather

than moving on to a richer experience, to a more abundant life. We all face that danger, but when backsliden, we don't look upon it as a danger. The Hebrew Christians faced the danger of falling short, failing to achieve their potential in Christian behavior and service. He exhorts them to press on. Hobbs explanation, I believe, is the most satisfying and consistent one. He is the author of an excellent book on the study of Hebrews formerly used in the study course curriculum of Southern Baptists. (Hobbs, *Studies in Hebrews*)

SUPPORT FOR THIS VIEW

I am sure that Dr. Hobbs does not stand alone in this explanation as evidenced by some of the commentaries. For instance, I would cite two that are available to me. In different ways and places they make relevant remarks that I believe are in support of this position. They also emphasize the need to press on, and to guard against sluggishness. We could stop being fruitful, which is what Christ has chosen us for, to "bear much fruit," "abiding fruit," that which has eternal results.

Other commentators did not believe that these verses described the whole Hebrew congregation. But it was a growing problem with some people in these verses. They understood that a person could not fall from salvation. They understood the impossibility of that happening. They knew that maturity was not automatic. It comes from attention and diligence to pursue Christian goals. Like Paul, they "pressed on for the prize." But some had become stagnant in Christian living. They are not even accused of backsliding. The writer understood this condition but did not deal with it in severity. Instead, he strongly exhorted pressing on for the only legitimate goal. Search the commentaries and you will discover that they agreed.

Other support comes from the affirmations of Chapter 6:13-20, which ends with God's promise, and God's oath, assuring us that we are His forever. He backs up His Word with an oath to strongly emphasize it. And God's character backs up His words.

The whole message of the Book of Hebrews is to the Jewish believers. The burden of the writer, whether Paul, Timothy, Barnabas or some other person, was to encourage the Hebrews move on to further growth, development, and faithfulness in the Christian life. "Let us draw near with a true heart in full assurance of faith, having our hearts sprinkled from an evil conscience, and our bodies washed with pure water. Let us hold fast the profession of our faith without wavering; (for he is faithful that promised;) And let us consider one another to provoke unto love and good works." (Hebrews 10:22-24) "Let us go forth therefore unto him without the camp, bearing his reproach." (Hebrews 13:13) "Let us offer the sacrifice of praise to God continually..." (Hebrews 13:15)

The illustration from the case of the children of Israel at Kadesh-Barnea is in support of this explanation. (Hebrews 3:8-11; 15-19) "When they stood off from God, it was impossible to renew them again unto a change of mind or attitude (a real sense of the Greek word translated repentance) with regard to their destiny, for God decreed that their carcasses should fall in the wilderness. Doubtless, they lived to see the day when they wished to repent of their sin of provocation, but God had already said that they should not enter into his rest." (Hobbs) At Kadesh-Barnea, Israel was "nigh unto cursing; whose end is to be burned" which is reminiscent of I Corinthians 3:15: "If any man's work shall be burned, he shall suffer loss: but he himself shall be saved; yet so as by fire." The Israelites were "nigh unto cursing." "But for the intercession of Moses they would have been destroyed and disinherited. Due to the priestly ministry of Moses, however, that generation escaped such a fate with only the loss of its place in God's redemptive mission. While a disobedient Christian group would be 'nigh unto cursing,' because of their high priest they would escape that fate to the loss of their fruit in redemptive witnessing." (Hobbs)

The illustration that follows this difficult passage is consistent with this view. "For the earth which drinketh in the rain that cometh oft upon it, and bringeth forth herbs meet for them by whom it is dressed, receiveth blessing from God: But that which beareth thorns and briers is rejected, and is nigh unto cursing; whose end is to be burned." (Hebrews 6:7,8) The reference, of course, is to the burning of the product of the land; the land itself was not burned." (Hobbs) God never meant for us to stand still in our Christian growth. Nor did he intend that we would cease from good works.

Hebrews 10:39 refers to the same situation, but instead of "fall away" it is "draw back." But the same conclusion is expressed by the writer, that of confidence that they would not "draw back unto perdition," and he identifies himself with them in their destiny as saved souls. This does not mean that there is no such thing as "drawing back' or "falling away." It is just that God takes no pleasure in it, and the writer, by exhortation and warning, seeks to avoid it in the Hebrew Christians. For the truly born again person there is no renouncing of faith, but there is backsliding and failure to press on in Christian development. This is what the writer was seeking to prevent. There is a condition of drawing back which was not fatal to their eternal destiny. It was not unto "perdition." But it was cold indifference to those things treasured by growing Christians. There is a real danger of drawing back to perdition when a person continually refuses to accept God's gracious gift of salvation. It is also a possible outcome when people hold tenaciously to false doctrines and "damnable heresies."

CONCLUSION

It is interesting that all of the unusual descriptions of Hebrews 6:4-6 have to do with the initial experience of the believer. It is also interesting to note that all of the definitions of apostasy distinguish between the experience of the unbelieving professor and the redeemed possessor of eternal life. It is also interesting to notice how many times the writer to the Hebrew Christians exhorts them to press on to maturity. It is this aspect that persuades me that the view expressed by Dr. Hobbs is the correct position, even though the "apostasy explanation" may be the easiest and simplest. The other explanations offered have no credibility. I can find no support at all from these verses for those who are looking for evidence that a person can lose his salvation.

If you have found that this passage in Hebrews is difficult to understand and explain, I join you. I trust this is a good example of a difficult passage. There are many more. We will not be able to cover them all, which is another reason why it is so important for all believers to press on to maturity in seeking the truth in understanding God's Word. I encourage all of you to do your own home work, to seek and compare Scriptures, in order to acquire further understanding.

CHAPTER 2

Difficult Sayings
of the Saviour

There are many things in the Bible that appear difficult to understand. That is true also of our Saviour's teachings. That is why it is wise to consider carefully the message intended for us as well as a clear understanding of what has been said, and why. Here again, it is helpful to consult the great commentators. Why do I say this? It is because they have spent the greater part of a lifetime respecting the authority of the Scriptures as well as commenting on them as a whole. This involves comparing Scripture with Scripture and "rightly dividing the word of truth." This is not to say they are infallible, but they can help us if we will let them. One I find most helpful is John Gill, the famous British Baptist commentator. I find him to be most thorough, direct and to the point, even if he is at times quite wordy. His commentary is available through the "E-sword" computer Bible Study program.

There are three subjects that Jesus dealt with that may have particular difficulties for many believers. At least that is what I have chosen for this chapter. You may have more than that, but these are the ones that stand out for me.

THE MATTER OF MOVING MOUNTAINS BY PRAYER

There are several passages where Jesus dealt with the fact that with God all things are possible. In Matthew 17, it is in connection with the miracle wrought by Jesus in casting the demon out of a child. The disciples wondered why they could not have done the miracle. "And Jesus said unto them, Because of your unbelief: for verily I say unto you, If ye have faith as a grain of mustard seed, ye shall say unto this mountain, Remove hence to yonder place; and it shall remove; and nothing shall be impossible unto you. Howbeit this kind goeth not out but by prayer and fasting." (Matt. 17:20-21) "This mountain" which He had reference to was probably the mount of transfiguration. He repeated much the same teaching in connection with the withering of the fig tree which caused the disciples to marvel at how quickly the miracle was accomplished. (Matt. 21:21, 22) The mountain here was probably the Mount of Olives, and for it to be cast the distance into the sea was difficult indeed. Mark also refers to this teaching in Mark 11:22-24. The ability to accomplish this miraculous feat is conditioned on a faith that none of us have, and cannot produce, and that is limited by the prayer that never fails: "Thy will be done."

Now let us get to the meaning of these words. There are three words that appear frequently in comments on all three of the subjects under discussion. They are "metaphors" and "figures." They are used "figuratively" as contrasted with "literally." These are literary devices used in communication and are frequent in poetry and narrative. If this seems strange to you, remember that Jesus was the Master Teacher and used them with ease to get his message across. Metaphor is defined as "a figure of speech in which a word or phrase literally denoting one kind of object or idea is used in place of another to suggest a likeness or analogy between them." (*Miriam Webster Online Dictionary*) A figure is usually one word in which the object is somewhat less than the truth it vehicles. With this understanding in mind, let us see how the commentators treat this subject. The promise of removing in this way can be accomplished with a strong faith. Who among us has this kind of faith? We continually have to confess and seek help with the prayer: "Lord, I believe, help thou mine unbelief." Paul also mentions the possible miracle of "removing mountain" which could only be accomplished by the miracle of faith. I believe the primary lesson our Lord was trying to teach us is He is the one that can do all things, which includes meeting our needs for strength and the needs of life. He has done it in the past, is doing it in the present, and upon His promise, will do it in the future. We need him for victory in the Christian life. He expands on these lessons clearer in other places. He has repeatedly made those promises in different places in His Word. So you might say that this was also the use of hyperbole, another literary device used in communication, which is exaggeration for effect and is not meant to be taken literally. It shows that nothing is impossible for God, but the limitations of our faith.

THE REFERENCES TO SELF-MUTILATION

These passages come in connection with offending little children. "Wherefore if thy hand or thy foot offend thee, cut them off, and cast them from thee: it is better for thee to enter into life halt or maimed, rather than having two hands or two feet to be cast into everlasting fire. And if thine eye offend thee, pluck it out, and cast it from thee: it is better for thee to enter into life with one eye, rather than having two eyes to be cast into hell fire." (Matt. 18:8,9) Mark records much the same teaching in 9:43,45,47. Matthew also records much the same teaching as Jesus deals with the lustful eye in 5:29,30.

This also should be understood and treated figuratively, not actually. I have heard of other religions actually cutting off limbs as punishment. They do this under their compulsion of a false religion. It is not practiced nor required in the Christian faith. Where the Christian faith prevails, it is not ever tolerated.

Obviously, these words are to be treated figuratively, not literally. Anything that is an obstruction to spiritual growth should be eliminated. As an illustration or object lesson, Jesus selected the hand, a prominent and necessary instrument of action, a precious possession for any individual. The follower of Christ should get rid of any action or attitude that is contrary to his Christian profession. Get rid of it if it is contrary to conscience and the commands of Christ. Nobody is actually required to pluck out their eyes or to cut off their hands. To do so would be sinful. God created them as a part of our being to serve Him. These teachings should be understood figuratively as a teaching lesson, aimed at our spiritual good. "So the figurative use of these expressions teaches the spiritually good, while not demanding self-mutilation." (Matthew Henry)

THE REQUIREMENT TO HATE FAMILY

In Luke 14:26, Jesus turned to the multitudes following him and said: "If any man come to me, and hate not his father, and mother, and wife and children, and brethren, and sisters, yea, and his own life also, he cannot be my disciple." (Luke 14:26) This has to be understood in light of what all the scriptures teach about loving family relationships. It cannot be in conflict. To hate anybody would be contrary to God's laws. We are taught to love our neighbors as ourselves and no man hates his own flesh. He does the best he can to preserve it. Now Jesus advances His teaching by bringing it to bear upon family relationships. He could not positively mean this literally, which would be in conflict with God's law, which He always observed. If they stand in the way of service and devotion to Christ, they are to be forsaken. If their stands are opposed to the honor of Christ, their interests should not supersede those of God. Nothing is to be preferred before Christ. Our primary love should be for Christ, love for family follows. Love for Christ involves and includes love for His Word. Love for ourselves should be last in this equation.

Mathew 10:37 does make the passage in Luke more clear and meaningful: " He that loveth father or mother more than me is not worthy of me; and he that loveth son or daughter more than me is not worthy of me." The purpose of these words was not to lessen the affection for spouse or children. We owe them that. No Christian parent would trade them for the whole world. It is the duty of parents to love them, to provide for them, to bring them up the right way. It is their duty to obey out of love and the understanding that discipline is for their own good. They are not encouraged to renounce a relationship with parents. The message of this passage is to teach that Christ is to always be above all other persons or things. This is consistent with all of the other messages of these difficult sayings.

I hope these brief interpretations and comments by the commentators have shed sufficient light on the subjects discussed as well as the practical use of metaphor, figure, and hyperbole in any communication. To force a literalness into these narratives produces far greater problems in understanding the difficult sayings of our Saviour. A further consideration is the fact of God in three persons, along with other believers, become the family for those who have never known a loving family or safety at home.

CHAPTER 3

Accursed From Christ

"For I could wish that myself were accursed from Christ for my brethren, my kinsman according to the flesh." These may seem like strange words coming from the great apostle. At least they cause us to stop and ponder what he was saying. I think these words by Paul may be the most difficult words for us to understand he has ever written. He had just finished the doctrinal section of Romans (Chapters 1-8) with a triumphant affirmation of his security in Christ. Now he begins the parenthetical section dealing with the role of Israel and the Gentiles in God's plan for the ages, (Chapters 9-11) before the practical section on the Christian walk (Chapters 12-16). His statement is intensely personal and mystifying, especially after his conclusion of Chapter 8. Just what he meant by being "accursed" is hard to understand. A favorite contemporary version does not help much. The one renders it, "accursed and cut off from Christ;" another states it, "I have actually reached the pitch of wishing myself cut off from Christ;" while some of the newer versions state it, "For I could even pray to be outcast from Christ myself;" and in a favorite contemporary version it is amplified simply as, "If there were any way I could be cursed by the Messiah so they could be blessed by him, I'd do it in a minute." None of these answer the question of what he meant by accursed. Was it in the sense of "excommunicate?" Was it in the sense of "desiring to be cursed?" Or was there some other meaning to this word? There have been several explanations of these words from different commentators. To better understand it, let us look first at a few obvious facts in his statement.

1. He does not say, "I do wish," but "I could wish." No person having committed his life to Christ would want to be "accursed from Christ." Nor was it possible to be so. Paul had just stated in the strongest terms that impossibility in a positive form in Romans 8:35-39.

2. His area of concern was for his "kinsman according to the flesh." He makes a distinction throughout the chapter of the natural and spiritual Israel. The kinsmen he is referring to are "Israelites; to whom pertaineth the adoption, and the glory, and the covenants, and the giving of the law, and the service of God and the promises." (Rom. 9:4) "For they are not all Israel, which are of Israel." (Rom.9:6) There is a spiritual Israel which is descriptive of the new covenant community of believers where there is neither Jew nor Gentile. Paul knew the ground is level at the cross.

3. His burden or concern was so great that he introduces his wish with several unusual affirmations: "I say the truth in Christ. I lie not, my conscience also bearing me witness in the Holy Ghost, that I have great heaviness and continual sorrow in my heart." (Rom. 9:1,2)

4. His reference to "my brethren" was not in a spiritual sense but as a pure natural sense as evidenced by his further statements. They were of the same nation and it was common among them to speak of all Jews as brethren, just as we refer to all believers as brothers and sisters.

Now we can proceed to look at several explanations of the phrase in question and seek to find the one that makes the best sense:

1. All the <u>punishment</u> due his brethren, because of his love for them, he wished to take upon himself, if possible, in order to atone for their sin. We can make several observations concerning his feelings, since he is not hiding them. They are highly exposed, in order to be clearly understood. His feelings were not hypocritical but sincere. He was willing to fore-go his own happiness, if it would benefit his brethren in any saving way. He was willing to cut off from his relationship with natural Jews, in order for them to be saved, if that were possible. He was willing to be regarded in a most unfavorable way by them in order to accomplish God's purpose. That would indeed be a personal punishment that he did not desire, but one which he would be willing to accept.

2. Some have rendered the words "I could wish" as "<u>I did wish</u>" in a reference to his unregenerate and unenlightened state. Others have softened the sense of the word "accursed." None of this expresses the deep compassion he had for his people. The whole sense of his discourse is future.

3. He could wish to be <u>excommunicated</u> from all of the privileges of his relation to the Christian community, if that in some way would result in their salvation. He had such affection for his brothers in the flesh that he was willing to endure excommunication in their interest. He did have a great love for the churches and the ordinances committed to them. But he was willing to be cut off from the churches as well as his brothers whom he also loved, in order that they could escape eternal punishment.

4. He "could wish" that a <u>great calamity fall upon him</u> to accomplish his desire. John Gill describes it as "I could wish that my dear Lord and Master, as if he should say, would appoint and order me to die, might this nation of mine but escape that ruin and destruction I see is, coming upon them, as a nation and a church; I could be content to die the most accursed death, and be treated in the most ignominious

manner, might they but be saved." In this sense, the word "accursed" has the idea of "doomed."

5. It was just a hyperbolical expression to qualify his intense love for Israel and his desire for them to be saved. It was more of a strong and indistinct emotion rather than a definite idea. Hyperbole is the use of exaggeration for effect and is not to be taken literally.

There is an element of truth in each of these explanations. In the first case, the explanation is only hypothetical. It would be impossible for Paul to atone for sin, but it does express the intensity of his love. In the second case, there is no evidence that he was referring to his past life, even though it does describe his estrangement from Christ. In the third case, it is true excommunication is descriptive of being accursed. "If any man love not the Lord Jesus Christ, let him be anathema maranatha." (I Cor. 16:22) The Jews practiced their own form of excommunication. In reference to the person of Jesus, their rule was: "If any man did confess that he was Christ, he should be put out of the synagogue." (John 9:22) The fourth case accurately describes the judgment coming upon natural Israel. The prophet Jeremiah stated that he did not desire "the woeful day." (Jeremiah 17:16) And it is probably true that Paul could wish to endure the described death, but it would not have changed the eternal decrees of the sovereign God. He did not desire "the woeful day" either, but knew it was coming. In the last case, it is true the biblical writers did use hyperbole, just as we do, as a legitimate tool for communicating ideas. However, to gloss over it as "just hyperbole" would be a mistake.

The explanation can best be discovered in the message of the whole chapter. His love and the desire for repentance and faith of his fellow Israelites was genuine and sincere. But there would be no salvation just because they were Jews. God had not discarded them, but "He came unto his own, and his own received him not. But to as many as received him to them gave he power to become the sons of God, even to them that believe on His name." (John 1:11,12) He is comforted by the fact they are not totally eliminated from the New

Covenant community. There would be an elect remnant of Jewish believers that would have the same experience of grace that he had experienced. They would be grafted into the good olive tree through their repentance and faith.

In conclusion, I would make several observations that might help us understand this statement. I realize there is no simple definition of "accursed" here, but I hope the following statements will enhance our understanding of this difficult passage.

1. <u>It was a heartfelt expression</u>. His deep and sincere compassion for the Israelites was very real and intense. So great was his concern, he used a threefold oath to affirm his wail of sorrow. They were his family. He was one of them. He was "a Hebrew of the Hebrews," from "the tribe of Benjamin." (Phil. 3:5) His statement might be compared to the intense desire of the Christian parent, desiring above all else to see the child come to saving faith. He might desire the greatest calamity, even an early death, so parent and child might be together in the eternal heavens. Paul was sincerely willing to endure the greatest misery in order to do them good. This was an unusual love.

2. <u>It was a hypothetical expression</u>. He knew full well he could never be separated from Christ. He had just expressed this in chapter 8. He also knew by divine revelation only a remnant of his own people would be saved. The hypothesis he projected did provide a basis for further argument and explanation of certain facts that could be very distasteful to his kinsman in the flesh.

3. <u>It was a hyperbolic statement</u>. Even though it was hypothetical it was stated in the highest possible form to describe his intense emotion concerning the fate of his people. What could be the greatest action the apostle could take to produce the desired end? Just what he stated, to be "accursed from Christ," although an impossibility for any born again person. Whether you look upon the "accursed" as excommunication

or desiring to be cursed, or doomed, how could it be expressed in stronger terms? It is reminiscent of Moses dealing with his people. When he reported to the Lord "the great sin" of the people making the golden calf, he pleads with God: "Yet now, if thou wilt forgive their sin--; and if not, blot me, I pray thee, out of thy book which thou hast written. And the Lord said unto Moses, Whosoever hath sinned against me, him will I blot out of my book." (Exodus 31:32-33) Moses could not be taken out of God's favor; only the people who had sinned.

CHAPTER 4

Succession or Perpetuity

Matthew 16:18

INTRODUCTION

We can learn something by referring to some of the reputable translations of this verse. Of particular interest to me are William Tyndale's Translation in 1526 and the Literal Version, copyright 1985 (LITV). This simple verse with just a few words has generated three theological controversies for those determined to understand its message. So this passage deserves its place in the most difficult passages of the New Testament. Sadly, many are not concerned. The first difficulty has to do with the identification of the "rock." The second is the nature of the church (*ekklesia*). The third is the question of succession or perpetuity. For the purpose of this chapter, I will focus mainly on the last two. My simple conclusion is that our Lord intended His church to be the institution to perpetuate the Gospel message, His teachings, and all of the sacred scriptures until He returned. We see it fulfilled in the world today. An understanding of the nature of the church is foundational to the question of succession or perpetuity.

THE IDENTITY OF THE "ROCK"

Debate has raged over this part of the statement. There are three proposed interpretations of the identity of the rock, none of which are entirely satisfactory. However, I will try to summarize them:

1. The rock is Peter. This appeals to the papal claim. It is the tradition and claim of the Roman Catholic church that Peter founded the church in Rome, served as its first pope, and was martyred there. But the New Testament refers only to some house churches in the city and there is controversy concerning Peter ever being in Rome. I can not imagine him in the role of pope when he referred to all believers as a "royal priesthood," "an holy priesthood." (I Peter 2:5, 9) The counter to this interpretation of the "rock" is based on the significance of the name Peter, being interpreted as "a little stone," and the "rock" being distinguished as a foundation.

2. The "rock" is Christ Himself. This is based on the Scripture that describes Christ as "the cornerstone." "The stone the builders rejected has become the cornerstone," and "A stone that causes people to stumble and a rock that makes them fall." I Peter 2:7, 8 (NIV)

3. The "rock" is the simple and comprehensive confession of Peter. The promise is made immediately after Peter's statement of faith. "Thou art the Christ, the son of the living God." (Matthew 16:16) Jesus regarded it as a powerful and summary testimony. This would include: the fulfillment of Old Testament Scriptures that the Saviour has come; the deity of our Lord; and by implication the whole Christian message. It recognizes Him as the Messiah- the fulfillment of Old Testament prophecy. It recognizes His deity as the Son of the living God. Mathew Henry attempts to reconcile the different views as he concludes that "the New Testament charter is here delivered to Peter as an agent, but to the use and behoof of the

church in all ages." He thus recognizes the importance of the confession and the person and work of Peter.

THE NATURE OF THE CHURCH

The emphasis here is on the "My." The Jews had their religious institution in the synagogue. The pagan world had their institution in the Greek assembly. Our Lord's institution would be different both in purpose and survival permanence. The triune God created the institutions of marriage, family and home. Jesus, during His earthly ministry created the institution of the church. You will notice from the translations, that two give meaning to the *ekklesia* as a congregation or assembly. The Literal Translation and Tyndale version give meaning to the Greek word whereas others have ignored its meaning and assigned the convenient word "church." It is unfortunate that most of the translators have used the word "church," a word derived from foreign languages with several different meanings, instead of a single meaning - congregation or assembly.

The simple word "church" (*ekklesia* equals assembly) has acquired various interpretations. In the Greek speaking world, the meaning is clear - a gathering of citizens for governing purposes. To many, or most evangelicals, it is equated with the kingdom of God or the family of God. The two are decidedly different. The kingdom is made up of all believers. The church is the permanent institution to promote the work of the kingdom. To others, an understanding that this word was used in the institutional sense retains the meaning of the word *ekklesia*. If this idea of an institution seems strange or difficult, consider some of these examples where I am reminded of how "church" as an institution is used in everyday language just as we would think of family, home, marriage, etc. in everyday conversation. Here are some examples I have heard or read recently:

"mellowing of the church"
"the persecuted church"
"the Eastern church"

"the Roman church"
"the American Church"
"the church covenant"
"the Christian's conduct in the church"
"the underground church"
"the doctrines of the church"

I can only understand these expressions or their characteristics in the institutional sense. They are general in nature and apply across the board. But the thing that settles it for me is our Lord's second use of the word in dealing with the problem of church discipline in Matthew 18:17: "Tell it to the church," which could only refer to a gathered congregation and not to any particular congregation, but the institution wherever it was manifested. It was a particular instruction with previous conditions. Our Lord foresaw the fulfillment of His promise in the future as the institution developed polity under the direction of the apostles. With our Lord's clarity on the matter, the choice is to either accept the word in its original meaning or introduce a new concept, alien to its meaning, of an unassembled assembly.

SUCESSION OR PERPETUITY

Having laid the foundation for this discussion, we come now to explore the subject of this chapter. In *Robertson's Word Pictures,* we learn that "Hades is technically the unseen world, the Hebrew Sheol, the land of the departed, that is death." So I understand the expression "gates of Hades" as a metaphorical expression to include all the forces of evil arrayed against the church. Communism, Islam, secular humanism or the spirit of anti-Christ (I John 4:7 and II John 7) will not prevail in the battle. They will not succeed in extinguishing the church. It will be here until Jesus comes again, observing the Lord's Supper "until He comes." (1 Cor. 11:26). A few statements may help us understand this issue.

1. Christ's church is one that corresponds to His message and the character of the New Testament churches. There comes a time

26

when a church ceases to qualify for that claim. The Laodicean church was one that He would "spew out of His mouth" unless they repented. The Jerusalem and Corinthian churches had problems but they worked them out. A church doesn't have to be perfect for Him to own it. Our own imperfections exemplify that truth.

2. Churches do cease to exist, but the institution does not. Persecution may wipe out an assembly. Economics and mobility may also have success. Mergers and closings may do the same. I was raised in a community where all I knew was the village Methodist Church. It was not until a few years ago in searching the community history that I discovered the existence of an earlier Baptist Church. I was pastor of a church that later merged with another and regrettably forsook their witness in that city.

3. A church does not have to be advertised as "Baptist" to be a New Testament Church. The simple definition of the New Testament church held by Baptists has been "a congregation of baptized believers." Many of our churches go by the title "community" but hold to Baptist beliefs and affiliation. Some churches in distant lands have strange sounding names to us but still hold to New Testament principles. Some Baptist churches in the States have forsaken Baptist distinctives and should not be considered a New Testament church.

4. All papal dissenting groups of earlier history do not necessarily qualify as New Testament churches. This is not to claim or assert that there were no individual congregations that might, regardless of the leader's role in describing the movement. Our Lord's assertion of perpetuity supersedes the speculations of the historians.

5. Nothing in our text requires a literal succession of church organizations, papal or otherwise. Denominations die, just as congregations do, when they forsake the Gospel message. Some mainline denominations today are experiencing decline and decay for that reason.

6. The promise is His institution would not cease to exist until He comes again. We see this played out in history. We have often heard that "the blood of the martyrs is the seed of the church." In our day we see the "house church" movement in areas of wide persecution. As new believers discover from the Scriptures their responsibility to confess Christ in baptism, they are not content until they obey and seek a like minded group. Regrettably, not all churches accept the responsibility to shepherd that new convert.

CONCLUSION

Succession implies an unbroken line of continuity. It is unnecessary and foolish for churches to make such a claim on the basis of this text or the findings of historical research. Perpetuity suggests the permanence of the institution – that it will not pass away. It did not disappear in the Dark Ages to be resurrected later. In all ages, there have been "congregations of baptized believers" somewhere in the world. This is clearly the intent of this promise. When new believers study the Scriptures they discover the marks or pattern for a New Testament church. They become aware of the necessity and importance of the *ekklesia*. The obedience of baptism is the ceremonial door into that fellowship. This is that fellowship that becomes Christ's *ekklesia*. I suspect as the missionary movement reaches the different people groups of the world, there will be congregations which treasure New Testament principles. Hopefully, as they grow in their understanding of the Scriptures, they will seek the New Testament pattern. I am reminded of Paul's persuasion that, "Neither death, nor life, nor angels, nor principalities, nor powers, nor things present, nor things to come, nor height, nor depth, nor any other creature" (Romans 8:38,39) could separate him from the Saviour's love. This is applicable to every true believer and the same words can be applied to the permanence of the church. None of these forces will prevail against the church.

CHAPTER 5

Cain's Wife

Someone wisely remarked that "it is a bad idea to be too much interested in another man's wife." Yet, here is a wife that is not named, who has been the interest of many for centuries. Some of the interest is from those who claim she could not have existed, and others' interest is to refute the skeptics and scoffers that have jumped on this subject to prove that the Bible is not literally and historically true. Apparently, they have not read the Genesis account very carefully. The account does record the history of Adam and Eve but does not name all of their descendants. Two children of our first parents were Cain and Abel. A family disagreement led to Cain killing his brother Abel. The account does not give their ages. It dwells upon the issue that divided them. Cain's offering in worship was from the "fruit of the ground" and Abel's offering was from the firstlings of his flock and of the fat thereof." God was pleased with Abel's offering, but as for Cain's offering He "had not respect." It ended with Cain killing his brother Abel. So the conjecture is since Adam, Eve, and Cain were the only persons on earth it would be impossible for him to get a wife as the Scripture mentions in Genesis

4:17. The whole premise of repudiating the Scriptures rests on this shallow and ignorant conclusion.

Sometimes in our search for truth, understanding things that are *not* said is as important as what is said. When that is coupled with the clear statements of scripture, we can come to a reasonable conclusion to resolve any difficulty. Certainly, what is not said in this narrative helps us understand the truth that God has revealed. Let us look for them here:

1. We are not told why God did not accept Cain's offering. We do know that it had to be the nature of the offering. The covering God had provided previously to Adam and Eve to cover their nakedness required the sacrifice of innocent animals. Their covering by leaves was indicative of self-righteousness. We know from other statements in the Scriptures that "without the shedding of blood, there is no remission of sins." (Hebrews 9:22) So that was the established standard. We are not told specifically that God had given Cain personally this requirement, but knowing the character of God it is reasonable to believe that He had.

2. We are not told when Adam named his wife Eve. We just assume that he did when God first gave her to him. But it could just as well have been when there were many descendants because she is called "the mother of all living." (Gen. 3:20) The title at least suggests the existence of a large family clan.

3. We are not told the ages of the two brothers when the family strife began or that they were the only children. They were quite likely mature adults with their own vocation—one a farmer, the other a shepherd. There could have been many children between these two who are brought into focus here for a specific purpose. Remember that Adam was 120 years old when Seth was born. To conclude that there were not other children born during that 120 years has neither been asserted or denied. But the likelihood is strong that there were many. At least one child comes into prominence after the slaying of

Abel. His name was Seth and he had the character traits of his father—"in his own likeness, after his image." (Gen.5:12) At this point, the genealogical information shifts to him because it was through him and his descendants that "men began to call upon the name of the Lord." (Genesis 4:26)

4. We are not told the names of the children born to Adam after the age of 120. We do know that Adam lived another 800 years and "he begat sons and daughters." Living that long and fathering that many children, it is quite likely that he had many daughters that Cain could have married. Since God had told man "to multiply and replenish the earth," we can reasonably presume that there were large families rapidly multiplying and the family tree would be difficult to construct. We should not think in terms of the practice in our contemporary culture of limited children. It wasn't too long ago that many of our ancestors had ten or more children. The point I am making is there was quite likely a large population by the time the fugitive Cain married, and they likely did not all live in Eden.

5. We are not told even that Cain was single when God banished him from Eden and "he dwelt in the land of Nod, on the east of Eden." (Genesis 4:16) All we are told is that "Cain knew his wife and she conceived, and bare Enoch." (Genesis 4:17) When he married, the name of his wife, and who her parents were, is not mentioned.

6. We are not told who the people were Cain feared would kill him. So God set a "mark" of divine protection upon him. (Genesis 4:12-15) Unless there were others living, how could they kill him? If you presume that Adam, Eve, and Cain were the only people left alive at this time, the threat of harm doesn't make sense.

So the age old question, "Where did Cain get his wife?" is not really the problem the skeptics and scoffers make of it. James Kennedy gives a brief but scholarly explanation of this issue in his book, *Skeptics Answered*, and he limits Cain's marriage to one of his sisters, which is entirely possible but not necessarily required:

> After he begot Seth, the days of Adam were eight hundred years; and he had sons and daughters.' It's quite obvious that Cain's wife was his sister. You might object, saying that it's forbidden in the Scriptures to marry one's sister. Yes, but we need to be careful about *ex post facto* laws-making laws after the event. The law forbidding such marriages was passed several thousand years later. You might point out, 'If one marries his sister, he is liable to have a very strange child.' That is true today, but evidently the gene pool was rich enough at the beginning not to constitute a problem. (p.28, 29)

From what the Scriptures do tell us, it is not necessary to conclude Cain got his wife in the land of Nod, even though it is the first place and time she is mentioned, and that is one possibility. Since we are not told when or where, we can speculate, for there are many possibilities. Nobody knows how many people were living at that time or how old Cain was when he married. He could have been like many men today, in no hurry to get married. Then he could have waited a small spell of about 700 years and married one of his brother Seth's great-great-great granddaughters. No doubt there were many to choose from. Evidently, it was not as much trouble for Cain to get married as for some folks nowadays. What is important is not when, where, and whom Cain married, but that we accept the narrative as historical. There is no reason to believe otherwise.

CHAPTER 6

Exploring A Divine Promise

"He shall give thee the desires of thine heart." (Psalm 37:4)

This is not a simple stand alone statement, as evidenced by the context, but it strikes at the very intense longings of mankind in relation to his Creator. If you could feast on this phrase alone, you would probably exult in liking of such a promise. It does recognize our dependence upon God for our everyday existence and that He is able to supply all of our needs, even some of our wants. His ability to supply our wants does not bind Him to that action. This promise is not unconditional and does have limitations. The context of this statement must be considered as well. "Delight yourself in the Lord; and He will give you the desires of your heart. Commit your way to the Lord, trust also in Him, and He will do it." (Psalm 37:4, 5) A few statements based on other biblical teachings might help us understand and appreciate this promise.

He expects us to ask. He delights when we ask. We are His children through faith in the Lord Jesus Christ. It is a natural situation in the human family for the child to express many desires. So it is with our heavenly father. He is pleased when we have that intimacy that causes us to "come boldly unto the throne of grace...and find grace to help in time of need." (Hebrews 4:16) The desires of the "heart" is an all inclusive statement, as the heart is used in the scriptures many times to cover the whole of life. Our Lord admonished us to "Ask, and it shall be given you; seek, and ye shall find; knock, and it shall be opened unto you: For everyone that asketh receiveth; and he that seeketh findeth; and to him that knocketh it shall be opened." (Matthew 7:7,8) Since "your heavenly father knoweth that ye have need of all these things," as revealed in Matthew 6:32, you may wonder: why ask? It is our duty to ask and God answers according to His infinite wisdom and loving will. There are some things that God bestows indiscriminately in His general mercies, "for he maketh his sun to rise on the evil and on the good, and sendeth rain on the just and the unjust." (Matt. 5:45) But He has special plans for those who know Him and trust Him. Ask Him; do not demand. You are the suppliant; He is the giver.

He does not grant our desires when we ask "amiss." He recognizes that not all of our desires are beneficial. We still have an evil nature as well as a regenerated, or renewed, one. He mentions the "lusts that war in your members." (James 4:1) God does not promise to us "the desires of our hearts" when we ask for things contrary to His will. "Ye lust, and have not, ye kill. And desire to have, and cannot obtain: ye fight and war, yet ye have not, because ye ask not. Ye ask, and receive not, because ye ask amiss, that ye may consume it upon your lusts." (James 4:2,3) The Psalmist also prayed: "Grant not, O Lord, the desires of the wicked: further not his wicked device; lest they exalt themselves. Selah." (Psalm 140:7)

He does not, and will not, abandon His sovereignty. All of our desires are not for material things. They might be for the salvation of a loved one or friend. They might be for physical healing. They might even be for a life and death issue. They may have to do with our spiritual warfare. God may have another and better plan for you. He does not abandon His plan and purpose. As mysterious as His sovereignty may be to us, it is a part of God's nature. Without it, He would not be God, unlimited in wisdom, and all powerful in order to carry out His eternal purposes. Perhaps when we use the words sovereignty of God, and attempt to apply it, we need to define the word simply as:

> The exercise of His supremacy. God is the one supreme and independent Being. He is the only one in all the universe who has the right and the power to do absolutely as He pleases. …He is the only one who has the right to act for His own glory. The sovereignty of God means that He does as He pleases, always as He pleases, and only as He pleases. God is in control of all things and all people, and is directing all things after His own will and to the praise of His own glory. He even makes the wrath of man to praise Him, and the wrath of man that does not praise Him, He does not allow. (Psalm 76:10) There is no alternative between an absolute sovereign God and no God at all. (C. D. Cole, *Definitions of Doctrine*)

Charles Spurgeon also treasured this promise on the basis of God's sovereignty, which he considered the most comforting attribute of God to His children. Those who cling to this doctrine under all the trials and adverse circumstances of life understand sovereignty is the only satisfactory explanation for those shunned adversities. They realize that God has ordained afflictions. Sovereignty overrules afflications as well, and God's sovereignty does and will sanctify any afflictions all for His glory.

He expects us to "delight" in Him. This is one condition for God to give us our heart's desires. We can be glad that there is a God who cares about us. He made us. He sustains us daily. Meeting our needs ought to be evidence that He loves. Why shouldn't we return that love? When we make God our heart's desire, He will give us our heart's desire. The basic desire of the heart of any good man is to love God and please Him. When that occurs, our adoration of Him increases. Our dependence upon Him is evident to ourselves and others.

I refer again to Spurgeon's support for the explanation of delighting in God. He felt that every attribute, name and deed of Jehovah God should delight our hearts. When this is true, men will not ask for anything which they know would displease God. Our will's are subdued to God's will which is infinitely wiser than our own. We can honestly say: "Thy will be done." For those petitions we believe to be His will, and for His glory, those He delights to receive.

He expects us to "trust" Him. This is hard to do in all the circumstances of life. Job's experience is the noblest example of a godly response to the worst of circumstances. In the midst of all his adverse circumstances, and his wife's counsel to "curse God and die," (Job 2:9) he resolved: "Though he slay me, yet will I trust in him." (Job 13:15) "We must do our duty (that must be our care) and then leave the event with God … and then trust in him to bring it to a good issue, with a full satisfaction that all is well that God does." (Matthew Henry) It is also of interest to note in connection with "trust," is the admonition to "do good." This helps us not to fret, but to leave the matter to God. The New Testament also emphasizes the same message in connection with saving grace and faith: "For we are his workmanship, created in Christ Jesus unto good works, which God hath before ordained that we should walk in them." Ephesians 2:10, James also emphasized works were an evidence God had done a work of regeneration. Without good works there is no visibility of change.

He expects us to "commit" our way to Him. This involves making Him our guide. It is submitting everything to Him. Our "way" is all of our choices, decisions and actions. When we accepted Christ as our Saviour, we lovingly, willingly accepted Him as Lord. That in itself makes Him our guide and our boss, if you will. He will work things out according to His own sovereign will. We may get discouraged, but as my daughter-in-law has said: "God's trains always come in on time." That is hard to believe. Lord, help my many times of unbelief. It is not ours to contrive all the means or to finish the expectation only God can perform.

Charles Spurgeon offered good advice: "Resign thy will, submit thy judgment, leave all with the God of all." It is then that the words of the old hymn, "Thy Way, Not Mine, O Lord," become meaningful and personal:

> "I dare not choose my lot,
> I would not if I might;
> But choose Thou for me, O my God,
> So shall I walk aright."

CHAPTER 7

A Sin Unto Death

I John 5:16, 17 speaks of a "sin unto death." This is probably one of the most difficult verses in the Bible to interpret. All of us are familiar with the precious promise of I John 5:14 and 15, and those verses are easy to understand. However, when we come to the next two verses, we struggle to understand the nature of the "sin unto death." We can easily associate "unto" as "leading to" or "results in." But we are not told the nature or identity of the "sin" mentioned, nor the nature of "death." It could be either physical or spiritual. Different translations can aid in our understanding, but in this case they do not help much.

I think the best way to approach the problem is first to identify the particular sin that results in death. There are several possibilities that deserve mentioning:

1. It is the "unpardonable sin" described by Jesus in the Gospel accounts. The difficulty here is it is not so characterized. John would be familiar with Jesus teaching on that subject and yet he does not relate this sin to that description. I suppose it could still be possible since he lived in the apostolic period where miracles gave credence to the Gospel message being established in the world. To commit that sin it must be

an intentional slandering of the Holy Spirit in the face of evidence to the contrary. There must be "light in the mind and malice in the heart."

2. It is the sin of "apostasy" described fully in this letter. An apostate person was one who had professed faith in Christ as Saviour but did not possess him in his real life. He could give assent to the truths of the Gospel and even have good intentions of someday trusting Christ. He might even know his need but procrastinate on that all important decision, then finally renounce his profession and spurious faith. Such a person has not been born of God, has never received the gift of eternal life, and repudiates all that he professed. John describes these people thus: "They went out from us, but they were not of us; for if they had been of us, they would no doubt have continued with us: but they went out, that they might be made manifest that they were not of us." (I John 2:19)

3. It is the continual practice of a sinful life style and rejection of all entreaties for repentance to the point of no probability of forgiveness. John Wesley felt that this sin was one God had determined to punish with death. There is sufficient evidence in the Scripture to illustrate this view. A case in point is that of Ananias and Sapphira in Acts 5:1-10. We are not told whether they were believers or unbelievers, but I assume they were believers since they were associated with the Christian movement. Their sin was hypocrisy, pretending to be more devoted than they actually were. Their sin resulted in immediate physical death. In I Corinthians 11:28-32, there is indication that the persistent carnality, while sitting at the Lord's table, resulted at times in physical death. "For this cause many are weak and sickly among you, and many sleep." (v.30) "Sleep" is analogous to death. Hymenaeus and Alexander are said to be "delivered unto Satan, that they may learn not to blaspheme." (I Tim. 1:20) Here, too, we are not told whether they were believers or not, but they made shipwreck of their faith. There are some sins which have an

adverse effect on other people and the spread of the Gospel may require severe discipline. The writer to the Hebrews gives a thorough explanation of God's chastening process which "afterward yieldeth the peaceable fruit of righteousness unto them which are exercised thereby." (Hebrews 12:5-11) God has promised that "as many as I love, I rebuke and chasten." He doesn't do this without a purpose. He first calls us to "be zealous and repent." (Revelation 3:19) There are times in the sovereign will of God that He calls a believer home, and that may be because of "a sin unto death."

Two other concerns need to be raised in discovering the truth of these verses. One has to do with the nature of death; the other has to do with the practice of prayer in the described situation. If you take the position it is spiritual death, you would have to conclude that it refers to the sin of an unbeliever. But this hardly makes sense, since the unbeliever is already spiritually dead and needs to be made alive spiritually through a new birth. If you take the position it is physical death, it can fit any of the three explanations offered; and it would be the most appropriate for the third explanation since the context deals with a "brother," a believer. Physical death here is in apposition to "life" that is physical and indicative of restoration and forgiveness upon repentance.

The encouragement to pray for the sinning brother to be repentant is incumbent upon other believers and carries with it the assurances of verses 14 and 15. In the first case, a Christian is in the act of sinning and continuing in that sin. Life was in danger of being forfeited when the believer's intercession changes the situation and outcome and obtains restoration. This is in accord with Paul's message to the Galatians. "Brethren, if a man be overtaken in a fault, ye which are spiritual, restore such an one in the spirit of meekness; considering thyself, lest thou also be tempted." (Galatians 6:1) Kindly reproof should accompany the prayer of intercession. Prayer, work, and witness can bring about the restoration of abundant living and forgiveness. The apostle does not expressly forbid praying for the second specific class of sinners. He expresses himself quite cautiously, because it is almost impossible to know when a man has reached that difficult point of implacable repentance and actually deserving of physical death. That is something only God can know. It is the final stage of divine discipline when God removes from the earth the backslidden and unrepentant person deserving only of physical death. There comes a time when God no longer hears the prayers for a sinning believer, nor does he expect us to pray, for the one whom He has determined that the judgment of physical death is due.

Conclusion: I have only indicated the possibilities of explanations one and two. Personally, I cannot make the connection between the unpardonable sin and the sin unto death. The apostle who must have understood perfectly Jesus' teaching about the unpardonable sin does not make that definite connection. In the second explanation of apostasy as the "sin unto death," it is buttressed by the fact that apostasy is of primary concern to John in his letter. However, he has dealt adequately with that problem and now deals with intercessory prayer. I do not believe that he moves from his focus on that "brother," or any believer, to a nonbeliever without making clear his intention. An apostate person has never been a "brother." I believe his message had more of the echo of Psalm 118:18, "The Lord hath chastened me sore: but he hath not given me over unto death." Or the message to Ezekiel: "But when the righteous turneth away from his righteousness, and committeth iniquity, and doeth according to all the abominations that the wicked man doeth, shall he live? All his righteousness that he hath done shall not be mentioned: in his trespass that he hath trespassed, and in his sin that he hath sinned, in them shall he die." (Ezekiel 18:24) Or Jeremiah's message: "Therefore pray not thou for this people, neither lift up cry nor prayer for them, neither make intercession to me: for I will not hear thee." (Jeremiah 7:16) Jeremiah recounted further the sins of his people and rendered the verdict from the Lord: "Thus saith the Lord unto his people, Thus have they loved to wander, they have not refrained their feet, therefore the Lord doth not accept them; he will now remember their iniquity, and visit their sins. Then said the Lord unto me, Pray not for this people for their good." (Jeremiah 14:10,11) I am sure that John was familiar with the fate of King Saul: "So Saul died for his transgression which he committed against the Lord, even against the word of the Lord, which he kept not, and also for asking counsel of one that had a familiar spirit, to inquire of it; And inquired not of the Lord: therefore he slew him, and turned the kingdom unto David the son of Jesse." (I Chronicles 10:13,14) John's description of "the sin unto death" is reminiscent of this event. This last explanation is also consistent with the fate of Ananias and Sapphira, the Corinthian Christians, and Hymenaeus and Alexandria, which have already been mentioned. It is sad but true, that a believer can get so far out of fellowship with God that other believers are reticent to keep praying for his repentance and restoration. It is also true that the ultimate chastening is physical death.

CHAPTER 8

"And the Graves Were Opened"

(Study Notes on Matthew 27:51-53 (KJV)

"And, behold, the veil of the temple was rent in twain from the top to the bottom, and the earth did quake, and the rocks rent, and the graves were opened, and many bodies of the saints which slept arose, and came out of the graves after his resurrection, and went into the holy city, and appeared unto many."

As I approach this passage, I am reminded of Rudyard Kipling's famous verse:

"I keep six honest serving-men
(They taught me all I knew);
Their names are What and Why and When
And How and Where and Who"

I think this might be a good way to discuss this passage, though not necessarily in that order. These details are included to such length only in Matthew's account of the crucifixion and resurrection. The startling rending of the veil is often discussed, but an explanation of the other details is overlooked. So an explanation with the "six honest serving men" may be a help.

What

The fact occurred. Many saints were resurrected and appeared to many in the city of Jerusalem. Jesus himself appeared to "above five hundred brethren," mentioned in I Corinthians 15:6. When and where that occurred we are not told. What is described here concerns the action of the first contingent of resurrected saints. An earthquake, opening of the select graves, and the appearance of those resurrected saints in the city of Jerusalem were a summary of the facts. The graves were near the city since no one was allowed to be buried within the city walls; hence their going into the city. John Gill explains all that occurred here "was a proof of Christ's power over death and the grave, by dying; when he through death, destroyed him that had the power of it, and abolished death itself; and became the plague of death and the destruction of the grave, taking into his hands the keys of hell and death." The whole account is to bear additional testimony to the reality of the resurrection of Jesus.

Who

Now this is a question that we cannot positively answer. Identifications have been offered in explanation such as the patriarchs, Adam, Noah and Job. That seems to me to be pure speculation because we want some answer. Some also speculated that it referred to Zechariah, John the Baptist, Simeon and Joseph. They had to be known to the people now alive for these identifications to make sense. Even others have contended recent martyrs in the cause of religion are meant. Some believe it was the Old Testament believers, but such a great many does not fit the details of the account, which indicates select saints. Whoever they are, they are viewed as trophies of Christ's victory over sin, death and the grave.

When

Mathew 27:53 - "And came out of the graves after his resurrection." The "When" is important in our understanding of these events. It is clear that the resurrection of these saints did not occur until after the resurrection of Christ. He raised Himself up as "the firstborn from the dead." There were those Jesus raised, such as Lazarus and Jairus' daughter, but they were to die later. The saints mentioned here, it was supposed, went directly to heaven, after finishing the ministry of making themselves visible, to give an additional evidence that the resurrection was real. It was a once for all resurrection for them, ushering them into the eternal realms. Others believe that they lingered on earth until the Lord's ascension into heaven, when He then took them with Him. That is admittedly hard to prove and can only be founded on supposition.

Where

The place is easier to ascertain, which is pointedly Jerusalem, **"the holy city."** It was still a holy city to the Gospel writers, even though it was a very wicked city that had rejected Christ and had Him put to death. I suppose it was holy to them because of the temple which was the center of Jewish worship, and the place of God's residence. The burying place of the Jews was outside the city, but they still revered the city for that reason. It was necessary in God's plan they appear to many of their acquaintances.

How

There were other factors which took place in connection with their resurrection, such as the quaking of the rocks, the rending of the rocks. They were simply brought back to physical life by the risen Christ at this time and in this way to become the "first-fruits of them that slept." They also became the pledge of a future resurrection for all.

Why

Some other facts bear repeating in answer to the why of this historical incident. It seemed wise, in the sovereign council of God, to establish further the historicity of the resurrection of His Son, as well as to give us some insight into the nature and surety of our own resurrection. Jesus, in His resurrection appearances, could appear without opening doors. We are told that we shall be like Him. So if we do not know all the mysteries of our resurrection bodies, we know they will be different and transformed.

CHAPTER 9

"He Descended Into Hell"

No, these are not the words from Holy Writ, but they are most notably familiar in "*The Apostle's Creed.*" This creed is shared by Reformed churches. It was not created or accepted in the time of the Apostles. In the history of the church, it dates at least a half century from the last writings of the New Testament. *The Nicene Creed* of 325 and 381 do not mention this particular phrase. *The Athanasian Creed* uses the same words. I remember the systematic repeating of these words in liturgical churches where I have visited, but never quite knew how to take this phrase, since it conjured up in my mind Jesus going to the lake of fire mentioned in Revelation 20. To be fair, we need to examine any Scriptural basis for this creedal statement. This is probaly the most difficult expression to explain. Let us try, anyway.

But first, let us acknowledge the contoversial nature of this statement. In earlier church history, there was not unanimous agreement to include this statement in the creeds. Even today, some denominations consider it optional. Some refuse to include it at all. John Calvin, in his *Institutes,* argues for admitting it to formal worship, on the basis it reflected a common belief on the part of the godly living in that time period. He felt it added meaning to the extent of the redemptive work of Christ. All of the church fathers mentioned it in their writings, although he admits their interpretations vary. He didn't feel it mattered as to the time, or by whom it was created.

Several views have been expressed by way of explanation:

1. The descent into hell represents the physical agony of death upon the cross. It was hellish in its pain.

2. It just repeats in different words the Gospel account about what had previously been said of his burial, because the word 'hell' is often being used in Scripture to denote a grave. Calvin conceded this point, acknowleding that the meaning of the word is true, and that "hell" is frequently to be understood as the grave. Others make the argument that the word "hell" is equal to Hades or Sheol, the collective abode of the dead. The Modern English Version renders it "he descended to the dead."

3. These words may suggest Jesus carried the sins of the world to hell. If that explanation doesn't work, try the suggestion that He carried the good news of deliverance to the godly dead still in the grave; for examples – Lazarus, Abraham, Isaac, Jacob, and the repentant thief, to announce the resurrection and events ending the world.

4. Still others believe the descent into hell accounts for the problem of God's justice by providing an opportunity for all mankind, in eternity, as well as in time, to hear the message of redemption from the living Word Himself. We need to remind ourselves that God's justice is ever on trial. It is one of His unchanging attributes. He has always been a just God.

5. Christ descended to the souls of the patriarchs who had died under the law, to announce that redemption was accomplished, and to free them from the prison where they were confined.

6. John Calvin, in his *Institutes,* looks upon this as an expression of the spiritual torment that Christ underwent for us. He felt it should be a great souce of consolation, that Christ would go

through the ultimate severity of God's judgment to appease His wrath - that He was doing battle with the armies of hell.

There are various Scriptures appealed to for support of one or another of these viewpoints. One group gives emphasis to the severity of Christ's physical sufferings on the cross, "the hellish pain" idea. Another group has reference to the "spiritual pain" of being forsaken by the Father, as He turned His back on His Son in order to punish sin. For example, His cry from the cross: "My God, why hast thou forsaken me?" We cannot belittle that aspect, but the expression we are examining has reference to a place, a location - hell itself. So we will examine the main Scriptures that might suggest support for this idea.

1. **Romans 10:7, "Or, Who shall descend into the deep? (that is, to bring up Christ from the dead.")** It is likened to Paul's use of a rhetorical questions in claiming his assurance of an everlasting salvation. There he answers his own question by strong affirmations, as he lists every possible force that were ineffective in separating us from God's love. There was not even a need to look for Christ in the grave. He has been ressurrected and ascended to the Father. We don't need to go to heaven to find Him either. He is here, invisibly, revealing Himself to His elect, as well as residing in heaven. He is the omnipresent God.

2. **Ephesians 4:8-10, "Wherefore he saith, When he ascended up on high, he led captivity captive, and gave gifts unto men. (Now that he ascended, what is it but that he also descended first into the lower parts of the earth? He that descended is the same also that ascended up far above all heavens, that he might fill all things.)"** The purpose of His ascension was to fulfill the type of the high priest entering into the most holy place; and to make intercession for his people, to prepare a place for His redeemed people which He had previously promised. He also "led captivity captive"

49

which can only have reference to His conquest of Satan. The resurrection and ascension completed that task. We were all captives of the Devil. Christ triumphed over him, and made us His own. Another explanation has been offered as to His descending into the lower parts of the earth. It was to emphasize His humiliation, coming from Heaven's glory with the father, being incarnated in a virgin's womb, humbling Himself to the point of "being obedient unto death," enduring the shame of the cross, being buried in a borrowed tomb. This God-man who created the worlds had "no place to lay His head, was made a curse hanging on a tree," and paying our sin debt.

3. **I Peter 3:19, "By which also he went and preached unto the spirits in prison."** Other difficult explanations have been offered for this verse as well. One is the contention that Jesus went by a special operation, such as the Holy Spirit striving with men, to enable men like Enoch to plead with "the spirits in prison." In other words, all of those who have gone before have had the gospel preached to them in their own day by the pre-existent eternal Christ through Noah and others.

We can explore the different views for insight, and we may come up empty. One interpretation of this verse views it as Christ going in His human soul either to preach to the demons and damned spirits, to let them to know that He has come, and thus fill them with dread and horror of what was yet to come in their eternal separation from God. It is maintained that He came to the prison to preach but didn't enter that horrible place. Only the spirits were in it. What could be the purpose in that? Their eternal destiny was fixed and the Scriptures no where hold out the hope of a second chance. That only happens before death. The purpose for such preaching is absurd, impracticable, needless, and impossible, because after death is the judgment, and at that point their destiny can not be changed. I would just mention one other view held by the Papists, which was that Christ went in His human soul to "Limbus Patrum," which was a real place, a prison where the Patriarchs and Old Testament saints were kept and He carried them with Him to heaven. Again, this is an impossible solution because when the patriarchs died, the soul was separated from the body and has already gone directly to heaven.

4. **Acts 2:27, "Because thou shalt not leave my soul in hell, neither wilt thou suffer thine Holy One to see corruption."** The Revised Standard Version, Phillips, and the New English Bible all translate hell here "Hades." It seems obvious from the context that "Hades" refers to the grave, not to a place of eternal separation from God. The prophecy was a description of death, burial and the historical resurrection of Christ, the Messiah. John Wesley pointed out that in the bodily death, the body went into the grave when the body was separated from the soul, but the invisible soul, when separated from the body, went into the heavenly realm referred to as Paradise. His body was not left in the grave, it did not suffer corruption.

Thus, my conclusion: It is not surprising that many churches who use the Apostle's Creed in their liturgy will not include this statement "he descended into hell." It is not a problem for non-liturgical churches who do not include as a part of their worship the recitation of a creed. But it doesn't hurt us to have some understanding of the history and basis for such a practice. To me, the extent of our Saviour's descent in the incarnation, humiliation and burial is all that is to be gleaned from these scriptures. In simple language, he descended all the way from glory to the cross, and a common burial. We do not need the fictitious and fabulous inventions that do an injustice to other scriptural teachings. Hell is not a temporary place of retribution but a place where there is eternal separation from God. So it makes no sense to argue that the descent of Christ extends to such a location. I agree with Matthew Henry: "He descended to the earth in His incarnation, He descended into the earth in His burial."

If you have difficulty understanding these explanations, I am sure that you are not alone. If God has not made plain the meaning of His Word, which regrettably, we humans have a tendency to mess up, you can resolve your difficulty by simply deciding that the secret things belong unto God. We welcome that course.

PART II

DIFFICULT DOCTRINES

CHAPTER 10

The Bible, Divorce and Remarriage

There are three areas of concern as we approach this subject of what Jesus and Paul taught about marriage, divorce, and remarriage. They are the exception sanctioned by Jesus; the exception of desertion, explained by the inspired apostle; and the "husband of one wife" qualification for the official church officers, pastors and deacons.

EXCEPTION ONE

There was a dispute among the Jews concerning Moses' teaching about divorce from Deuteronomy 24:1-2: "When a man hath taken a wife, and married her, and it come to pass that she find no favour in his eyes, because he hath found some uncleanness in her: then let him give her a bill of divorcement, and give it in her hand, and send her out of the house. And when she is departed out of his house, she may go and be another man's wife." One group's position was that it meant "for every cause." The other group said it was only for the cause of adultery. They were both wrong, but that did not deter the pharisees from trying to ensnare Jesus. His answer goes back to the creation of man and woman and asserts the permanency of marriage. (Matthew 19:4-6) Divorce was not approved of for "every cause," nor was it narrowed to adultery, but specified "fornication," the word that included other sexual sins such as incest, perversion, and infidelity. It was a word for all kinds of sexual uncleanness. The ISV uses "sexual immorality." Phillips translates it "unfaithfulness." The RSV and NEB translate it "unchastity." Fornication breaks the oneness of man and wife. One can be "one flesh" with only one person. Paul warns against becoming one with a harlot. (I Cor. 6:16) The innocent party may either forgive and reestablish the physical oneness, or else may regard the physical union with the guilty party broken. In such case, following the severing of the legal contract, God regards the marriage as put asunder. The innocent party is free to remarry; the guilty party is not. That is the provision clearly stated by Moses in giving the laws concerning divorce - "she may go and be another man's wife." Death dissolves a marriage and divorce dissolves a marriage. Even allowing for this exception, Jesus explained that Moses made it because of the hardness of their hearts, not because God desired it. "What therefore God hath joined together, let not man put asunder." (Matthew 19:6)

This raises another question suggested by Matthew 19:9, "Whosoever shall put away his wife, except it be for fornication, and shall marry another, committeth adultery: and whoso marrieth her which has been put away doth commit adultery." Again the translations vary. In Matthew 5:32, the unwarranted divorce "causeth her to commit adultery." This effect on the wife is variously described in different translations as "making her an adulteress," "involves her in adultery." This stigmatism would naturally occur since the only provision for divorce was fornication. This was the implication of the unwarranted divorce. The statement of our Lord was mostly a commentary on the injustice of the man divorcing his wife "for any cause." Since divorce dissolves the marriage, she is free to remarry and probably will. Some have deduced from this statement the concept of "the state of living in adultery." Nothing is said here concerning the lifelong relationship. Adultery is not a state but an act. The "oneness" has been dissolved and "oneness" with another created, regardless of how sinful or despicable that might be. Nothing is said or implied that when the spiritual, social, and physical union has been broken that the innocent party cannot or should not remarry. Jesus' words make it clear that the one who divorces his wife outside of this exception and marries another commits an adulterous act, and the one who marries the wife he has discarded commits adultery, since in God's eyes he (the divorcer) is still married to her. Matthew19:9; 5:32. He does not say the wife has committed adultery. The sinful act of the man divorcing his wife for other reasons than fornication puts her in the unavoidable position of being viewed as an adulteress. She is called an adulteress, stigmatized as such, not because of blame, but because God's ideal, the oneness of one man with one woman has been broken. The man who marries the victim, the innocent party, is said to commit adultery. I believe the same principles may apply when the roles are reversed, although Jesus did not deal specifically with those circumstances. Jesus was taking the side of the wife and defending her. She was so often the victim. This outlook may not be evident or true in our culture today but it was clearly the implication of the law of unwarranted divorce. Note that this is true for the "any cause" divorce. It is not true where the exceptions are the deciding factor, "the just cause." Closely associated with this teaching by Jesus was his assertion in Matthew 5:27: "Whosoever looketh on a woman to lust after her hath committed adultery already in his heart."

SECOND EXCEPTION

There is one other exception given by Paul in I Corinthians 7:10-16. A summary teaching of this passage reveals: The wife is commanded not to "depart from her husband." If she does, she is to "remain unmarried" or be reconciled to her husband. The husband is commanded not to put away or desert his wife. If a Christian has a wife who is an unbeliever and wants to preserve the marriage relationship, he is to honor that choice. The same is true when the roles are reversed. The reason given is in verse 16. By staying together, there may be a union of faith. This can come about by example and faithful witnessing. If it is impossible to save the marriage under these circumstances, he allows for a separation: "But if the unbelieving depart, let him depart. A brother or a sister is not under bondage in such cases: but God has called us to peace." (v.15) This is a specific case as already described. If the unbeliever is offended by the spouse's Christianity and refuses to preserve the marriage, choosing to depart, that is desertion, is the only other exception along with fornication.

There are several factors which we should remind ourselves and others. Being the deserter is not for that person a breach of the marriage contract. The deserted person may remarry and probably should for human reasons. To cause the desertion is a breach of the marriage contract. For the innocent party, in remarriage the deserted gets out of subjection to the deserter. When the unbeliever desires to impart, the believer is not bound to force the unbeliever to stay in a marriage of continual discord.

HUSBAND OF ONE WIFE

In I Timothy 3:2, Paul sets this forth as a qualification for both a bishop (pastor) and a deacon: "A bishop must be blameless, the husband of one wife..." and in verse 12, "Let the deacons be the husband of one wife...." Some people insist that this must be taken literally and prohibits a divorced man from serving in these offices in the church. If this view were practiced consistently, no unmarried man would qualify, and certainly not a woman because she could not be a husband. In all probability, Paul was not married and so far as we know the same would apply to Timothy. So they would not meet the qualification described. I know of no record where the early church put this interpretation on these words. Herschel Hobbs held that Paul meant, as did A. T. Robertson in *The Expositors Greek Testament,* "what is here forbidden is bigamy under any circumstances." And on verse 12, it refers back to this comment on verse 2. Matthew Henry takes these verses to mean "not having many wives at once.'"

These passages have a historical background and should be interpreted in light of the practices involved in marriage at that time. Gentile pagans might have many wives at once, which was true also of many of the Jews. So we are brought back to Jesus' teaching about the exception of fornication (sexual immorality of any kind). It is inconceivable, in allowing for this divorce, that a person should be deemed unqualified for these offices when this is the case. I would also make the same application for divorce because of desertion. Divorce dissolves the marriage and nowhere is remarriage under these circumstances forbidden. The original needs of creation are still there; man needs a helpmate and it was not good for man to be alone. The law provision allowing "when she has departed from the house, she may go and be another man's wife" was not abrogated by Jesus or Paul. So, there is no question in my mind that the requirement was dealing with the problem of bigamy, not divorce and remarriage.

Because of the erroneous interpretations of these passages, many good and qualified men have been rejected and subject to a handicap in potential service, while others who have never been involved in a divorce, but have had sexual partners outside of marriage, are never subjected to the same scrutiny.

A TESTIMONY

As a young minister, I started my pastoral ministry with a resolve never to marry a couple where there had been a divorce. I was never comfortable with that decision and decided to rethink the whole matter by a closer study of the Scriptures. This commitment deepened after watching good men being embarrassingly rejected during the election of deacons procedures, all of the time ignoring the exception rules of Jesus and Paul. I finally concluded that my responsibility and privilege was to help people rebuild their lives, rather than treat them as second class church members. This was not done indiscriminately as to reward divorce. Divorce always metes out its own measure of pain and grief for all that are even near it. Many divorces do take place outside of either of the two exceptions. But divorce is not an unpardonable sin and should not be treated as such. Repentance and forgiveness are possible for the offender. Forgiveness and restoration are appropriate for friends, family and the church fellowship. Again, we can learn from Jesus' example with the guilty, convicted, adulteress woman in John 8:3-11. Her accusers wanted her stoned, but Jesus' verdict was: "Neither do I condemn thee, go and sin no more." For that reason, and as a result of my studies on this subject, I offer my summary findings on the problem.

SUMMARY STATEMENTS ON BIBLICAL TEACHING CONCERNING DIVORCE AND REMARRIAGE

1. The General Law of marriage in the Bible sets forth God's ideal, permanency of marriage. Romans 7:2; Matthew 19:3-8

2. Jesus and Paul both gave exceptions to the general law. Jesus approved the Jewish divorce for the cause of fornication (sexual immorality) in Matthew 5:32, 19:9. He did not put a lifelong penalty of no remarriage on the law of right cause. He stood for the needs and right of the woman. Paul approved the Greek divorce where a Christian partner is deserted by an unbeliever. I Corinthians 7:15. The Greek divorce bill embodied the same dissolution of the marriage as did the Jewish divorce.

3. Dissolution of marriage. Death dissolves marriage. Divorce dissolves marriage. Dissolution carried the right of remarriage. Separation-divorce was the exception in a particular circumstance and problem dealt with by Paul in I Corinthians 7:10, 11.

4. Divorce on a Biblical basis. Jesus restricted divorce to one cause – it had been lawful for every cause in the minds of many of the Jews. Where there is a valid ground for divorce, the marriage is dissolved for both parties. The guilty party must take the blame before God for the dissolution of the marriage.

5. <u>Divorce without Scriptural grounds.</u> When the divorce takes place and is not based on the Scriptural exceptions, the marriage is still dissolved. The guilty may experience forgiveness upon repentance and confession to God just as for any other sin. It is not the unpardonable sin and should not be treated as such. Where God forgives, we are to join in real forgiveness of others and ourselves.

6. <u>Rules that have not been voided by divorce.</u> Divorce does not alter the general law stating man's need for a help-meet or God's recognition of that need. It is still true, "to avoid fornication, let every man have his own wife, and let every woman have her own husband" and "it is better to marry than to burn" with passionate desire in an unmarried state. I Corinthians 7:2,9

7. <u>The husband of one wife</u>. This qualification for pastors and deacons must be understood in terms of the historical background, and forbids bigamy under any circumstances. A blanket policy of rejecting people for service upon the basis of <u>any</u> marriage failure at <u>any</u> time has no justification in the Scriptures. It should be only one of many criteria considered in enlisting and placing Christian servants. We cannot be indifferent or permissive concerning sinful attitudes and actions involved in divorce, but when family stability has been established and forgiveness experienced, divorce should not be a judgment factor.

8. <u>Redemptive attitude needed</u>. Divorce – the breaking of God's ideal for permanency in the marriage relationship has its own built-in penalty in the form of personal, family, financial and social heartaches. The church should not add to this judgment but provide a healing, forgiving and accepting ministry to the wounded parties, without condoning divorce apart from the biblical exceptions. If this were to occur, it would be a reversal of some strongly held erroneous beliefs, which would also contribute to healing for the individuals as well as the church as a whole.

CHAPTER 11

Doctrines of Grace

Introduction: This chapter examines one of the most disputed beliefs of the different denominations of Christianity. The doctrines of grace should not be that hard to understand and accept, but they are. This chapter seeks to examine the main points of Calvinism and how they have influenced the historic confessions of faith. I will limit it to *The New Hampshire Confession of 1833*, *The Westminster Confession* and *The Baptist Faith and Message*. These Confessions are not creeds, such as the Apostles Creed, that are recited as a part of liturgical worship, but are statements of commonly held beliefs by different communions. The doctrines of Calvinism are generally held by the reformed churches and others, and are often summed up under the acrostic TULIP. So we will pursue our subject under these headings. Although I know nothing of a creed or confession that outlines their beliefs in this way, I do recognize it as a reformed system of doctrine. It exalts God and the salvation He gives freely to man. Many that are not associated with the Reformed movement prefer to call them the doctrines of grace rather than Calvinism. We accept their conclusions without the nomenclature. I am not including the Scripture references given with each confession, but they can be viewed with the whole confessions on the Internet.

1. **Total Depravity**. This is not to be understood as the inability to do something moral, but refers to the inability of man to do anything to save himself. The simple statement of Romans 3:10,11 ought to settle that. Nobody can deny they teach that all fall short of God's requirements, because of their sin, and that there is none who seek God. That is what total depravity is all about. That nature still resides in regenerated persons. We may not like this picture, but it is accurate.

   The Westminster Confession held that by man's fall into sin he lost his original righteousness and became dead in sin, acquiring an evil nature, and passed that corrupted nature on to his posterity, as well as progresses to actual transgressions. The Westminster Confession sums it up well in it's statement: "Man, by his fall into a state of sin, has wholly lost all ability of will to any spiritual good accompanying salvation: so as, a natural man, being altogether averse from that good, and dead in sin, is not able, by his own strength, to convert himself, or to prepare himself thereunto."

   The New Hampshire Confession held that man created in holiness, by a voluntary transgression fell into the sinful state, became inclined to evil, and fell under the just condemnation without any defense or excuse.

   The Baptist Faith and Message held that man was a special creation of God in an innocent state, who in the beginning was endowed with the freedom of choice and all men now inherit an evil nature because of that choice to sin. "Therefore, as soon as they are capable of moral action, they become transgressors and are under condemnation. Only the grace of

God can bring man into His holy fellowship and enable man to fulfill the creative purpose of God."

Commentary: On this point, as well as two others, the confessions are in essential agreement. They are not contending that people are as bad as they can be, but they are spiritually dead, and sin has affected every part of man's being, including the mind and the will, so much so, that man cannot do anything to save himself. Salvation must be by grace alone and faith itself is a gift of God. Through the fall, man is enslaved by sin and the devil. Total depravity has reference to man's natural condition apart from any restraining or transforming grace.

2. **Unconditional Election** is not as difficult to understand as it is to accept. Natural man rebels against such a concept until transformed by grace. It only falls to reason that, if man has no ability to save himself, then God must do it. Thus the explanation of unconditional election follows. The Scriptures are clear on this matter and the great confessions are also clear, and they have stated their conclusions.

   The Westminster Confession makes clear that those predestined unto eternal life, have been chosen by God, not the other way around. The choice was made in eternity by a sovereign God. Predestination was not predicated on anything in foreseen faith or anything God foresaw we would do, but was of His will, of His good pleasure, for His everlasting glory, and to bestow His gracious undeserved favor. He has not decreed anything on the basis of what He saw in the future.

   The New Hampshire Confession is in essential agreement specifying it is the eternal purpose of God to save, regenerate and set apart those chosen ones. He also ordains and encourages the means to accomplish it. It excludes boasting, and promotes humility, in trusting God for every action, not one's own efforts: "It is the foundation of Christian assurance; and that to ascertain it with regard to ourselves demands and deserves the utmost diligence."

The Baptist Faith and Message, in asserting God's purpose of grace, adds that God's election to save sinners is consistent with man's free agency, and that it is a grand, holy and wise display of the sovereign goodness of our Creator, Saviour, Redeemer.

Commentary: Unconditional election means that one's election cannot be dependent or contingent on any spiritually worthy actions or merit one may commit. This point in Calvinism asserts that God predestines to choose to soften the heart of certain fallen individuals, and to liberate them from spiritual death. This he does, not because of any merits or demerits in them, but from His own sovereign will and purpose. If He did not do this, there would not be anybody saved. The Bible nowhere declares His purpose to save everybody but to call out a people for Himself. God is the one gathering His elect. You will notice also in all of the confessions the "use of means" to accomplish His eternal purposes. I do not see any support in these confessions for Arminianism from either Baptist or Reformed groups. Nor is it accurate to state that they have not historically affirmed this position. An examination of the Scriptures cited in these confessions should affirm and confirm their support now. To me, this is a pivotal point in these confessions and Calvinism. If you accept this statement of belief, the other points logically follow, whether detailed or explained thoroughly through the Confessions.

3. **Limited Atonement.** This doctrine seems to be the hardest to understand and accept in the "tulip." So, we will begin the task of unraveling it from man's conceptions. The accompanying Scriptures are clearer than the confessions, but we will not shun their aid to understanding. It, along with the Scriptures state simply and clearly that God will not fail to accomplish

His eternal purposes. Those He has called, His Elect, have been redeemed and belong to Him. He justifies, regenerates by the power of His Spirit, sanctifies, and keeps by His power.

The Westminster Confession is in agreement with the aforementioned summary: "Wherefore, they who are elected, being fallen in Adam, are redeemed by Christ, are effectually called unto faith in Christ by His Spirit working in due season ... Neither are any other redeemed by Christ, but the elect only." It is the atonement - the death of Christ, that was designed for the elect believers.

The Baptist Faith and Message makes clear a truth that many want to avoid when it describes particular redemption by the words "who by His own blood obtained eternal redemption for the believer." How much clearer can you get? The limits could not be plainer.

The New Hampshire Confession adds their own brief statement in describing the atoning work of Christ, "by His death made a full atonement for our sins." Brief does not make the statement invalid. There can be no debate about the meaning of "our." The redemption is limited to the believer.

Commentary: Limited Atonement or "particular redemption" is difficult to understand or explain for the following reason. No one can limit the potential extent of Christ's entire life, suffering, and death. If everyone believed, they would be the beneficiary of His complete redemption. But they do not believe, apart from God's electing grace, and the convicting, regenerating power of the Holy Spirit. Although His atoning death is infinitely intensive in saving power and thus unlimited in that sense, it is not infinitely extensive. It is not universal in the extent of its saving power. While everyone shares "provisionally" in the atonement of Christ, it is only the believer (the elect) who experiences the full benefit of His redemption. This is where the "limited" feature comes into play.

You will notice the Baptist confessions make only brief mention of the atonement, but it has reference to believers. Nowhere will you find universal redemption or salvation affirmed in the confessions.

4. **Irresistible Grace** describes the overpowering work of God's Spirit in effecting what He has ordained. It is not describing the "how" God works. It just affirms that none can stay His hand. The natural man is not hungering to know God. He wants to get as far away as He can. He is not even seeking God. God is seeking him, and even decrees the means for drawing him to Himself.

   The Westminster Confession helps us understand that "drawing" work. In conversion, God frees the sinner from the bondage of sin and enables him to freely choose Christ as Saviour, giving him a new nature while not obliterating the old. Man can still will to do evil. It is God that overcomes all enemies to His eternal saving purpose and continual offering of loving obedience. When God purchases eternal redemption, He is not conquered. He continues to govern by His Spirit. He continues to freely and lovingly make intercession for His erring children. He is the one that enables us in our Christian walk.

   The Baptist Faith and Message adds descriptions of God's work in regeneration, producing a change of heart and receiving the gift of faith. It is the work of God, not man's in producing repentance and faith, which are inseparable experiences in the experience of saving grace. Man's part is in the confession of accepting Christ.

Commentary: The Reformed Confession does a better job here of explaining the all-sufficient grace through their treatment of "effectual calling." It is the logical outcome of Total Depravity and Unconditional Election. If you accept these, then you should easily understand that God is not going to fail or fall short of His eternal purposes. It is true that there is a general call to salvation, but it is just as clear that there is an effectual call. The general call is eminently resistible, insufficient, and ineffective to give life to a dead soul or liberate an enslaved heart. Here is where God's regenerative acts comes into play. This special call or act is invincible, overpowering all opposition. There is no need to add anything to this all-sufficient grace such as human cooperation. If you do not accept that, you do not know God's character very well.

5. **Perseverance and Preservation of the Saints** is a subject that describes God's keeping power. On this point Calvinists and Arminians are more in agreement. The Arminian works to keep himself saved. The Calvinites works because he is saved and obeys willingly and lovingly. The Arminian has extreme difficulty in resolving his dilemma concerning the new birth experience and the desire to be preserved in that state. Baptists, on the other hand, are prone to gloss over sufficient understanding, to rest in their affirmation of "the eternal security of the believer." God continues to forgive sin, never forsakes or renounces His redeemed child, but chastens to accomplish repentance.

   The Westminster Confession properly emphasizes God's part in completing the redemption process, which only ends in glorification. Man can fall under the Father's displeasure, but He does not cast them out. He works in their lives to renew their faith, to confess their sin, and bring them again to repentance. That part of repentance is a continuing exercise.

   The New Hampshire Confession also explains that real believers do endure unto the end. They cannot do otherwise because they are a new creature in Christ. This is not true of superficial professors and it is true that a special Providence that watches over their welfare. This confession also makes plain that the believer is kept by the power of God. That is eternal security. And that is God's work. He does the keeping.

The Baptist Faith and Message describes perseverance in terms of not falling from a state of grace. The believer may fall into sin through neglect and temptation. We may even bring reproach upon the cause of Christ, and temporal judgment upon ourselves. I might add, these are not happy experiences, yet they do not cancel God's power to keep us unto salvation.

Commentary: On this last point there is general agreement. Baptist's favorite designation is "eternal security," but more than that, it involves the perseverance and preservation of the saints. The true believer (saint, elect) will persevere in his faith. The professing Christian may apostatize when there has been no regeneration. Whenever God creates faith in the human heart, He will sustain that faith, that saving relationship with Christ, causing us, by His grace, to persevere in faith. All of the confessions recognize the continued existence and struggle with sin, a backsliding, but never an undoing of regeneration.

CHAPTER 12

Concerning The Kingdom

I attended college where the motto was "For Christ and His Kingdom." I did not give much thought to the message it conveyed. I knew that they taught a Christian world-view in every academic discipline or I would not have attended there. I do not recall their explaining what they wanted to emphasize with the slogan, but I had my mind on other things. Later in life, I became friends again with a colleague I met in Bible college, who was a pastor in a Southern Baptist church. For some reason, the subject of the kingdom came up, and I was surprised that he was repulsed by any other concept than the millennial kingdom. He had been so indoctrinated in dispensational theology that he could not conceive of the kingdom in any other way. So I think a brief biblical survey is in order and might be helpful.

A FALSE NOTION

The following is an outline of C.I. Scofield's argument for a distinction between the kingdom of heaven and the kingdom of God and the position of those who follow his dispensational teachings concerning last things. I am summarizing his teachings here not as an endorsement, but as the expression of a false notion, which will be dealt with in equal criticism. Everything I present will be a rebuff to the following teaching:

1. The kingdom of God is not the same as the kingdom of heaven.
2. The kingdom of God is universal, comprised of angels and the saved of all ages; whereas the kingdom of heaven is Messianic with the purpose of establishing the kingdom of heaven on earth.
3. The kingdom of heaven is not only made up of professors but also includes true Christians and just professors; whereas the kingdom of God is entered by the new birth and is forever. He builds his case on a further fuzzy misunderstanding of the message of the parables, while ignoring that in the same teaching and events they are used interchangeably in the different Gospels.
4. The kingdom of God is inward and invisible; whereas the kingdom of heaven is organic and is yet to be manifested in all of its splendor on the earth.
5. The kingdom of heaven merges sometime in the future with the kingdom as they are established forever. (c.f. *Scofield Reference Bible,* 1917, p. 1003. Footnote #1 to Matthew 6:33)

Not everybody is buying this scheme. I don't see eye to eye with Scofield on many things, including his doctrine of the kingdom and his view of last things. The writers on the following sites in this chapter share some fair, if harsh, criticism. The writer in the following paragraph obviously had been quite steeped in dispensationalism but his comments are quite helpful. The words on his website are discerning: "Each time I have read a book or sat in a class that describe standard distinctions between the kingdom of God and kingdom of heaven, I left unsatisfied. I always felt each time I have read a book or sat in a class that describe that the teaching was guilty of proof-texting." (*Learn the Bible website*)

A PRESENT REALITY

Dr. David Naugle gives us a good and sensible definition of the kingdom and they introduce us to the present reality of the kingdom: "The Kingdom of God is the rule or reign of God. It is not ... heaven, or moral reform,... It is God's sovereignty in action against all the evil in the world! It came into the world in Christ. It is both present and future. (*The Colson Center website*)

R.C. Sproul contends that "there is not now, nor was there ever, a kingdom on earth and a kingdom in heaven, because...We do not wait for His inauguration. All authority in heaven and on earth has been given to Him...Now He sits at the right hand of the Father...Now He is bringing all things under subjection. ...This is not merely a future hope, but a present reality. ...It is, however, becoming more visible, more manifest." (*The Ligonier website*)

And John Piper writes: "The King sits at the Father's right hand and reigns now until all his enemies are under his feet...The King's victory over Satan is now already ours as we use the sword of the Spirit, the Word of God." (*Desiring God website*)

The following verses contain Jesus' teaching on the nature of the kingdom which John the Baptist proclaimed to be at hand. They pretty well describe the present reality of the kingdom of God during Jesus' earthly ministry. He further described its nature extensively through parables. That is the kind of kingdom we have today, and which Jesus mentioned twice in what is commonly called the Lord's Prayer, "Thy kingdom come" and "Thine is the kingdom."

In Luke 17:20 and 21, Jesus used several phrases to describe His kingdom. In various versions we learn that it "does not come with observation;" It is "in your midst," "it is within you," does not consist of eating and drinking but of righteousness and peace and joy in the Holy Spirit. Other expressions are used in connection with different events, such as when Jesus cast out demons. He described it as the "kingdom of God has come upon you." And for the Jewish nation, which had rejected Him, it would be "taken from them."

Nobody has to wonder where the kingdom is from these expressions. It is obviously not equated with the institutional church. It is not just a matter of the heart and a spiritual life as held by Pietists. It is not social reform as held by theological liberals; it is not a future messianic kingdom consisting of 1000 years literal reign. From Jesus' own words, it is clear that it refers to the active, dynamic exercise of God's rule, authority, dominion, and power in the world! The teaching of the New Testament is clear: The Kingdom is both "already" but "not yet." It has come, and yet it is coming. It is both present and future." (see the *Colson Center website*, article by Dr. David Naugle)

Before we leave these scriptures, there is one statement in Matthew 8:12 that might be confusing, unless you accept the plausible explanation that the children of the kingdom are the Jews that persist in unbelief. *"The children of the kingdom shall be cast out;"* that is the Jews that persist in unbelief, even though they were by birth *"children of the kingdom."* From all of the Scriptures, it is clear that the kingdom of God is invisible and we enter it by the new birth. We enter the kingdom when we respond to God with faith and allegiance. It is also clear that the sovereign rule of God is evident in all things.

After we enter the kingdom, we come under the authority of the King and we then seek to live in a way that is reflective of that kingdom. *The Baptist Faith and Message* provides an excellent definition and description of the kingdom of God, together with the scripture references that support it. "The Kingdom of God includes both His general sovereignty over the universe and His particular kingship over men who willfully acknowledge Him as King...The full consummation of the Kingdom awaits the return of Jesus Christ and the end of this age." Please refer to the *Baptist Faith and Message* Confession itself for supporting Scriptures and a brief discussion of the responsibilities of Kingdom subjects. Notice carefully that the present kingdom has two aspects. One is the sovereign reign of God over all creation, and the other is the spiritual aspect that relates to the new birth experience and the guarantee for such the entrance into the eternal kingdom.

A FUTURE PERMANENCE

The kingdom is forever. It is eternal. This is the "not yet" aspect of the kingdom. There is only one kingdom. When a person enters the kingdom of God, in its invisible sense, they are guaranteed eternal life, which is God's gift to the repentant believing sinner. That is the permanence for us. Even C.I. Scofield has to admit, in his convoluted way, the future permanence of the kingdom. R.C. Sproul reminds us again: "We do not wait for His inauguration. All authority in heaven and on earth has been given to Him...Now He sits at the right hand of the Father...Now He is bringing all things under subjection. Now He is conquering all His and our enemies...This is not merely a future hope, but a present reality." *(Ligonier website)*

CONCLUSION

In conclusion, I am amazed that any Bible student could advance such a theory as promoted by Scofield, especially since there is a sensible and obvious explanation in the fact that the words are interchangeable in the Gospel accounts. Since Matthew was writing to the Jews, who still held God in such reverence that they would not speak His name, Matthew sometimes substituted heaven for the name of God. When the Kingdom of heaven and the kingdom of God are used in reference to the same gospel account, they are the same. Compare Matthew 4:17 with Mark 1:15, and Matthew 10:7 with Luke 9:2.

I am a lot more satisfied with the explanations of three respected Bible scholars in the writings of Sproul, Piper and Naugle. I have often heard it said that Jesus was a prophet, priest and king, but king was always in the future. There has never been a time when he was not King. He was born king, was crucified as king, and reigns today as king and will reign that way forever, as "King of Kings and Lord of Lords." (I Timothy 6:15) So now Christians worldwide can joyfully sing the words of Handel's *Messiah*:

Hallelujah! for the Lord God omnipotent reigneth.
The kingdoms of this world is become the kingdoms of our
Lord, and of His Christ: and He shall reign for ever and ever.
King of Kings, and Lord of Lords.

CHAPTER 13

Free-Will Fiction

One of the dictionary definitions of fiction is "something accepted as fact for convenience, although not necessarily true." It is in this sense I am using the word here to describe free will. Free will is defined as "the freedom of the will to choose a course of action without external coercion but in accordance with the ideals or moral outlook of the individual." Philosophers and theologians have struggled with this concept for centuries and there appears to be no consensus. If you make a Google search on the Internet, you will find a host of different opinions and explanations and you can search the technical and philosophical solutions to the problem. In this chapter, I am concerned with what the Scriptures teach concerning the will of man and the will of God in the salvation, conversion, and regeneration experience. Is the human will absolute, or such that it can determine the right course of action apart from any external involvement? The will is defined as "the power of making a reasoned choice or decision of controlling one's own actions."

The scriptures do present a general appeal in such statements as "And whosoever will, let him take the water of life freely." (Revelation 22:17) "For whosoever shall call upon the name of the Lord shall be saved." (Romans 10:13) These statements indicate that a choice has to be made. However, they do not go into other Scripture passages which make plain to us the work of the Almighty in exercising that choice. To neglect that is to make man and his reason the determining factor alone. Perhaps this is what people have in mind when they assert: "God votes for you; the devil votes against you; and you cast the deciding vote." The idea may have appeal to the natural man, but it fails to give glory to God who is the all-powerful agent in the salvation experience. If it were not for the divine initiative, the convicting and regenerative work of the Holy Spirit, there would be no conscious deliberative decision to choose Christ. If you go back to Luke 14 and read how a certain man made a great supper and sent out his invitation to the guest list, he found that "they all with one consent began to make excuse." So the lord told his servant to "Go out into the highways and hedges, and compel them to come in, that my house may be filled." (v.23) He not only prepared the feast, and made the invitations, but also filled the chairs. So it is with our Lord; He paid not only the sin debt with His death on the cross; He makes the general invitation; but apart from the divine initiative, there would be no response.

In the John 8, Jesus discusses with the Jews their spiritual bondage, in spite of their relationship to Abraham, and explained that "Whosoever committeth sin is the servant of sin." (v.34) "If the Son therefore shall make you free, ye shall be free indeed." (v.36) He further explained their spiritual bondage, disregarding their claim that they were the children of Abraham. He asserted, "Ye are of your father the devil, and the lusts of your father ye will do." (v.44) Every unbeliever is in this spiritual bondage and needs to be set free by the risen Lord. In II Timothy 2, Paul speaks of those who "oppose themselves" and God, giving "them repentance to the acknowledging of the truth" and recovering men from "the snares of the devil, who are taken captive by him at his will." (v.25,26) Hebrews 2:15 speaks of delivering those "who were all their lifetime subject to bondage." Ephesians 4:8 describes the ascended Christ as the one who "led captivity captive." Ephesians 2:1 describes the lost man as "dead in trespasses and sins." None of these verses indicate to me the reality of what some people call free will.

When we come to the other side of the picture, we discover the sovereign God who does have a free will and who inserts Himself into the lostness of man, and does something about it. In describing the new birth, John states: "Which were born not of blood nor of the will of man, but of God." (1:13) James states the same message: "Of his own will begat he us with the word of truth, that we should be a kind of firstfruits of his creatures." (1:18) Paul explains more fully the divine side of our redemption: "Having predestinated us unto the adoption of children by Jesus Christ unto himself, according to the good pleasure of his will. To the praise of the glory of his grace, wherein he hath made us accepted in the beloved." (Ephesians 1:5) "Having made known unto us the mystery of his will, according to the good pleasure which he hath purposed in himself." (Ephesians 1:9) "In whom also we have obtained an inheritance, being predestinated according to the purpose of him who worketh all things after the counsel of his own will." (Ephesians 1:11) "For it is God who worketh in you both to will and to do of his own good pleasure." (Philippians 2:13) You will notice in all of these passages the emphasis is on God's will, not ours, and that is "to the praise of the glory of his grace."

Sinful man will not naturally come to Christ. To describe them as sinful is not very appealing to them. You have to show men they are lost in order to persuade them to accept Christ as their sin-bearer. They do not have any innate hunger or thirst for righteousness and forgiveness. Any such inclinations must be produced by a loving, caring God. It is in this way that He draws. These are wrought by God and in His hands they are most effective drawing lost men to Himself. The stubborn will, without experiencing any force upon it, finds that God makes the will willing to be saved. He is simply drawn to Christ by the cords of God's love. (Philippians 2:13)

The *Westminster Confession,* which expresses the view of Reformed Theology, describes the will of man as "natural liberty." In the "state of innocency," man had "freedom," and by his fall into a state of sin, has wholly lost all ability of will to any spiritual good accompanying salvation: so as, a natural man, being altogether averse from that good, and dead in sin, is not able, by his own strength, to convert himself, or to prepare himself thereunto… When God converts a sinner, and translates him into the state of grace, He frees him from his natural bondage under sin; and, by His grace alone, enables him freely to will and to do that which is spiritually good; yet so, as that by reason of his remaining corruption, he does not perfectly, or only, will that which is good, but does also will that which is evil… The will of man is made perfectly and immutably free to do good alone in the state of glory only.

The New Hampshire Confession speaks only of "free agency." *The Baptist Faith and Message* (SBC) uses the same term and also explains: "In the beginning man was innocent of sin and was endowed by his Creator with freedom of choice. By his free choice man sinned against God and brought sin into the human race."

The scriptures never use the term "free will" or "free moral agent." It seems to me that "freedom of choice" would be the best way to describe this attribute of man as created and after his fall into sin. This freedom does not imply moral ability. We are free to fly to the moon, but we do not have the ability to do so unless we are financially able to secure a ride on the space shuttle. We are free to accept or reject Christ, but only by the decretive will of God and the work of the Holy Spirit do we make the right choice. This is in accord with the Scripture that distinguishes between a general and specific call. "For many are called, but few are chosen." (Matt. 22:14) The decretive will of God is that attribute by which He determines and executes future events. We do not have the moral ability apart from the divine initiative to make the right choice. So this idea of "free-will," generally accepted as fact for convenience, is in reality fiction.

In spite of this, many people will have trouble with II Peter 3:9: "The Lord…is not willing that any should perish, but that all should come to repentance." There is a difference between "willing" and the "will" that determines and executes future events. "Willing" just expresses desire or pleasure in the outcome. God's very nature is to wish that sinners will repent and turn to Him. They do not because they are dead in their own trespasses. God has done His part, loving them, sending His Son to pay for their sin, in a terrible death by crucifixion. He has loved them with an everlasting love. It is no delight to Him when men choose eternal wrath rather than His forgiving love. Yet, God has given all men space and time to repent out of His forbearance and long-suffering. When they are fixed on a terrible destiny of their choice, He will deal severely with them. The reason He has not hastened His coming is that He has not yet gathered all of His elect.

CHAPTER 14

Unraveling Tongues

I guess this subject would be one of the most controversial among evangelical Christians, or at least misunderstood. I will again use the famous verse of Rudyard Kipling to discuss the subject, but not necessarily in the same order.

> "I keep six honest serving-men
> (They taught me all I knew);
> Their names are What and Why and When
> And How and Where and Who"

WHAT

Let us begin with WHAT. The first thing needed is a definition. What are we talking about? The *International Standard Version* (ISV), the *Literal Translation of the Holy Bible* (LITV), and the *Contemporary English Version* (CEV) translate the relevant passages "languages." If this were accepted and understood, it would eliminate much of the confusion concerning the subject. Robertson helps us define the meaning of "tongues" with his observation on the Acts account: "**With other tongues** (*heterais glōssais*), other than their native tongues. Each one began to speak in a language that he had not acquired and yet, it was a real language and understood by those from various lands familiar with them. It was not jargon, but intelligible language." (*Robertson's Word Pictures*)

WHERE

Let us begin with the Acts account, where the advent of the Holy Spirit takes place. An unusual phenomena takes place with that tremendous event. (Acts 2:4) Men were filled with the Holy Spirit to the point they were accused of drunkenness. The witnesses did not know what to make of men speaking to them in their language. They did not recognize the power of God on clear display among them, so they had a hearty debate among themselves to try and determine what this was all about. If you would research the different versions, you would discover at least some of them translated the glossolalia as "languages." The response of the crowd gives evidence of that. As the apostles spoke, the mixed multitude had quickly gathered and were startled because each one heard the disciples speaking in his own language. Their conclusion recognizing their different nationalities was "Yet we all hear them using our own languages to tell the wonderful things God has done." (Contemporary English Version)

WHY

Why this extraordinary and sensational gift which others desired and perhaps tried to imitate with "ecstatic utterance?" There is evidence in the Corinthian Church that this was true. We do not know whether Paul is referring to the languages of men or angels to this practice. (I Corinthians 13:1) It was really the least gift being treated as the greater one, because the Corinthians put undue emphasis on this gift. I have no doubt that many today desire this gift above others, to be or seem more spiritual. There are better ways to become Godlike. God has given the resources. Try prayer, studying the Word and another language in order to share the Christian message worldwide, and public worship. "Ecstatic utterance" can be whipped up, taught how in classes or by individuals, or even be demonically and falsely inspired. But the genuine spiritual gift is divinely bestowed. "The more excellent way" is love.

WHO

I have reserved discussion of who for the Corinthians. It is here that Paul deals with the problem within public worship. Right after asserting the superiority of love and the superiority of the gift of prophecy over the sensational, the apostle exhorts: "Keep on pursuing love, and keep on desiring spiritual gifts, especially the ability to prophesy." (I Corinthians 14:1)

Paul testifies of his qualifications in dealing with the problem in I Corinthians 14:18,19: "I thank God that I speak in other languages more than all of you. But in church I would rather speak five words with my mind to instruct others than 10,000 words in another language." He shows by these words that He did not belittle the power of speaking in a foreign language. "How many" languages could Paul speak? In all probability, he had such a gift, though he doesn't tell us. He did not treat it with pride, but with thanksgiving. It was a tool he exercised in world evangelism. He did claim the ability to speak more foreign languages than any of the Corinthians. But he felt that there were more valuable endowments than this. "How many" languages could Paul speak? He has no-where told us.

> "It is reasonable, however, to presume that he was able to speak the language of any people to whom God... called him to preach. He had been commissioned to preach to the 'Gentiles,' and it is probable that he was able to speak the languages of all the nations among whom he ever traveled. There is no account of his being under a necessity of employing an interpreter

wherever he preached." (*Albert Barnes' Notes on the Whole Bible*)

HOW

In I Corinthians 14:26-28, Paul lays down some rules for the practice of languages in public worship:

1. Everything must be done for building up the saints spiritually. He was not censorious of their practices but recognized they needed to be controlled. Sharing a psalm, testimony, teaching, another language or interpretation of that language was not wrong in itself.
2. If anyone speaks in another language, only two or three at the most should do so, one at a time; and somebody must interpret.
3. If an interpreter is not present, the speaker should remain silent in the church and speak to himself and God. These instructions limit the role of language speaking in public worship and put the brakes on the artificial gift, as well as explain the role of other the other gifts.

WHEN

The gift of languages took place in public worship. It was when the whole church had gathered. A problem became obvious and Paul had to deal with it. He described the problem in I Corinthians 14:23, and explained why it was a serious problem. It was because the scene of everybody speaking in another language would be so confusing that an unbeliever or educated person in attendance would think they were "out of their mind." Paul gives a more intelligent prescription for orderly worship. "Let all things be done decently and in order." (I Corinthians 14:40) Key instructions are given for the exercise of these gifts, summarized as is taught in I Corinthians

14:1-5: Keep on pursing spiritual gifts, they are a gift of God. Keep on putting the priority on love and the ability to prophesy. These provide encouragement and comfort as well as instruction. They build up the whole congregation, whereas exercising the gift of languages is not actually speaking to others because that person is actually speaking to himself and God, who alone understands, because he is talking secrets of the Spirit.

What place do languages have then in the church? Very little because it is highly regulated by Paul at "the Lord's command." The reason for this command is because it is a sign to unbelievers and the worship service is mainly made up of believers. That is still true today, no matter how hard the effort made to bring unbelievers in for the revival service. See I Corinthians 14:26-33 for Paul's prescription for an orderly service, and the reason given is "God is not a God of disorder but of peace." Public worship should always be performed and managed so as to be understood by a hungering congregation. It is the church's responsibility to see to it "that all things are done decently and in order."

CONCLUSION

I know I have not exhausted the subject, but I am registering my convictions as a result of my study. It is clear to me the "tongues" are languages, not ecstatic utterance and should be so rendered in all of the translations. It could have eliminated the confusion of meaning for all of us. It is also clear that the "languages" are a spiritual gift, not something to be taught. Ecstatic utterance can be taught and even conjured up, by humans or by the enemy. All that is required is to set your mind in neutral and your tongue in high gear and you will end up with a bunch of gibberish where Satan can come in with his message. We can safely conclude that if all of the rules for the exercise of this gift were observed in public worship, the abuse of this gift would disappear.

There may be occasions in the missionary movement where similar episodes are evident, and where the gift is exercised for the purpose of God's Sovereign way to evangelize new peoples. Some see that in I Corinthians 14:22, in view of Paul's admonition - "Forbid not to speak in languages." Some have also noted Paul's words in I Corinthians 13:8: "Love never fails. Now if there are prophecies, they will be done away with. If there are languages, they will cease. If there is knowledge, it will be done away with." (ISV) I would grant that the gift of languages is rarely and sovereignly given in civilized countries since it is a sign to give credence to the gospel and was so employed at Pentecost and in the house of Cornelius. But that does not mean that it is confined to the apostolic age when the gospel was introduced to the masses, and now is abolished forever. Perhaps the reason for this position is that the interpreters don't want to be associated with the abuses of this gift. The abolishment would be true of prophecy and knowledge as well because they are indicated in the very same verse. We need both of them to proclaim the good news of what Jesus has done for us. We need languages and proclaimers in order to evangelize the peoples of the world.

I fear also that, in certain cases, the exhibition of "tongues" is thought to be a sign of superior spirituality. This is possible in cases where a substitute gift of ecstatic utterance is pursued. Paul recognized that problem in the Corinthian church, which is why he lovingly exhorted them to pursue prophecy. Prophecy has as its main purpose to proclaim truth, which every member should do at least in the personal witnessing situation. Evidence that some of the Corinthians were subject to the attraction of this sensational gift is found in I Corinthians 14:4; where the egotist is on display, "he builds himself up."

Once the KJV translated "languages" as " tongues," many later accepted that translation as a matter of convenience, I guess. This is what the KJV translators did at the king's instruction, when they avoided translating the Greek word for "immerse" to a transliterated word "baptize," and other translations followed suit.

CHAPTER 15

Healing Today

In this area of Christian practice, there is always the temptation to let the love of money rule. Many in the practice of faith healers let this be a snare into foolish and harmful lusts, where it has destroyed their integrity as a person professing to teach God's Word. The love of money, the root of all evils, becomes evident in their lives as they stray from the faith and "pierce themselves through with many sorrows." It is only a matter of time, and the long-suffering of God, before the greed catches up with them. They would do well to constantly heed the warning of I Timothy 6:9-10.

INTRODUCTION

My calling in life has been to the gospel ministry. So you would expect me to study, observe, and evaluate teachings and practices in this area. This will be the basis of my thoughts on this subject. The idea that persons are healed by prayer and divine intervention, often referred to as a miracle of healing, is not a recent development. The practice of an individual claiming that the healings were a result of his or her actions have been popular throughout my lifetime.

Miraculous recoveries have been attributed to the techniques of the individual healer. All of these practices have been lumped together as "faith healing" miracles. I have also observed throughout my ministry that people are more concerned about their body than their soul. To discuss this subject, we have to deal with several different areas.

DIVINE HEALING

All real true healing is of God. He made our bodies and our minds. All healing is Divine, whether with or without the use of medicine. God's usual method is to bless the means that are used; but sometimes He heals without medicine, but not at the hands of quack healers. Sometimes He heals in answer to prayer. Sometimes He doesn't. It may be God's sovereign will for the affliction to remain for some reason beyond our limited understanding. If so, it will be for God's glory. When we claim the promise that the apostle Paul did when the "thorn in the flesh" was not removed, he learned that God's grace was all-sufficient, and that God had a sovereign purpose in his keeping the affliction. God is always in control, working all things after the counsel of His own will.

COUNTERFEIT HEALING

Some years ago a great theologian, B.B. Warfield, wrote a book entitled *Counterfeit Miracles*. It is still available and is a valuable resource in the study of this subject. The theological convictions of Warfield dictated that he recognized the use of means to effect healing. He did not exclude God in the process, but honored Him who has appointed means. To look to means and disregard God would be a mistake. To look to God and disregard means would be an equal mistake. Warfield held to the biblical view of trusting God and using all the means He has put at our disposal.

There have always been, from New Testament history until the present, the magicians and sorcerers who worked counterfeit miracles. In Acts 19:11-19, we meet some of them. Seven sons of Sceva, wandering Jews, practiced the exorcism of demons. They met the apostle Paul who had the apostolic gift of healing and they desired his gift. When they tried to practice it in his name, and in the name of Jesus, the demon possessed man attacked them violently and they fled from the house naked and bruised. This occurred because they did not believe in Jesus but simply tried to use his name in a magical way.

PSYCHOSOMATIC ILLNESS

"Somatoform disorders are characterized chiefly by physical symptoms without a clear medical or biological basis, but which instead are thought to arise from some deeper psychological source." Steve Balt, MD, current Editor-in-Chief of *The Carlat Psychiatry Report (TCPR)*. (*Thought Broadcast website*)

The dictionary describes psychosomatic disorders as "characterized by disruption of normally occurring mechanisms of the body which involve the nervous system, physiological functions, endocrine system and the immune system. One's environment, social setting, upbringing, genetics, and coping mechanisms play an important role when an individual is faced with a psychosomatic situation." (*International Encyclopedia of Rehabilitation*) Somatoform disorders deal with the tremendous power of the mind that influences thoughts, feelings and behaviors.

Psychosomatic illness is observable and can occur in both individual and group cases. I can think of two such instances in my ministry. A lady member of our church was admitted to the hospital for some unknown malady. The lady that shared the room with her was to have surgery. In discussing the symptoms with her, she came to identify them with her own and insisted on the same surgery. The doctor performed the demanded surgery and came back to report the results, that there had been no need for the surgery. I was in the room. The husband angrily refused to accept his report. On another occasion, we were hosting a group of teenagers at the Ridgecrest Baptist Assembly for youth week. One teen got sick and then another, and another, each having sympathy symptoms even though they were not sick. So we spent the night taking them to the infirmary on unnecessary trips. It was all a case of identifying with the one sick person in mind matters.

A competent Christian Counselor can help a person find and deal with the mental, emotional and spiritual roots of these physical symptoms. Psychosomatic illness has some medical overtones to it. For the understanding of the problem and the expertise to deal with it, I would refer you to a competent christian counselor. I presume that is part of the counselor's training. I think this may be where hypochondria also comes in. It is defined by the Mayo Clinic: "When you have hypochondria, you become obsessed with the idea that you have a serious or life-threatening disease that hasn't been diagnosed yet. This causes significant anxiety that goes on for months or longer, even though there's no clear medical evidence that you have a serious health problem." I guess most of you have seen such persons, or those who seem to enjoy having an illness to talk about. An imagined illness has driven many to the television healers. There was a lady in one of our churches who repeatedly claimed she had an ailing back. She drove many miles to an Oral Roberts crusade and successfully got in the prayer line, and claimed healing when she returned. In another week she was, once again, complaining of an ailing back.

TV HEALERS

I haven't met or heard of one true faith healer. In the following notes you will detect an element of cynicism and disgust mixed with fact, so I have to concur with most of the facts posted in different places on the Internet. The reason there are no legitimate faith healers and so many claiming the gift of healing is that faith healers make a lot of money and the healing business has become a money making scam, and the source of many heresies afflicting the church. It is time to rebuke them.

Another money making feature of the healing crusades is obtaining a mailing list for the constant exploitation of the gullible.

A mail order business for the sale of books and tapes is a lucrative business as fake healers make it to television for advertising. That also facilitates the appeal for love gifts as well. They will even exploit the rebates from tax returns, estates, and Living Trusts, from trusting, unsuspecting people.

One of the tools of the fake healer is to give the impression that they are speaking to God and hearing from Him personally, a gift that differentiates them from others. They can do this because God has anointed them for the work, therefore what they do has to be legitimate. Another tool is the management of who gets in line for healing. You might also search the Internet for evaluation of some of the well known healers, e.g. Katherine Kuhlman, Peter Popoff, Kenneth Copeland, Benny Hinn and others. They made a name for themselves and a bunch of money.

MIRACLES TODAY

Yes, there are miracles today. To me, electricity, telephones, computers, air flight, etc. are all miracles. If you have a secular humanistic world view you may look upon these as just the upward strivings of man; God had nothing to do with because He doesn't exist. The Christian world view recognizes that God our creator controls all of human history. In 1844, Samuel Morse, painter turned inventor, sent the first telegraph message "What hath God wrought." It would be great if people had the same spirit of appreciation for these tremendous advances in civilization which are works of the Almighty. God hides himself so silently and wondrously when these kinds of miracles occur.

There are other kinds of miracles today. Physical healing is not at the hands of the healer's demands, but by the will of our sovereign God. To me, God's healing by the use of natural means is just as much a miracle as one with supernatural natural means. The real ones, without the use of means may be so hidden but greatly appreciated by loving family and friends because they are sovereignly distributed. Even in the days of the apostolic gift of healing, healings were limited.

In the days of public miracles, Paul had the gift of healing, but he could not always exercise that gift. "And God wrought special miracles by the hands of Paul: So that from his body were brought unto the sick handkerchiefs or aprons, and the diseases departed from them, and the evil spirits went out of them." (Acts 19:11,12) We have read of special miracles God wrought through the hands of Paul as the human instrument in healing, This was not always the case. We read of his friend Trophimus being left by Paul at Miletum sick. We do not know the nature of his sickness. We do know that Paul didn't heal him. (II Timothy 4:20)

Isaiah prescribed a fig poultice for Hezekiah's boil and promised that he would recover. God blessed the use of means to the end that he was healed. (Isaiah 38:21) Paul prescribed a little wine for Timothy's poor stomach. (I Timothy 5:23)

There is also evidence of supernatural healings in India and other parts of the world today that give credence to the Christian Gospel. These healings are happening because of fasting and prayer. That reminds us of the words of our Lord in Mark 9:29: "This kind can come forth by nothing, but by prayer and fasting." These words were uttered to explain His healing of of the demon possessed man.

There is one miracle that I consider the greatest of all that is so often overlooked. It is the miracle of regeneration. How is it accomplished? God raises up somebody to share the good news of what Jesus did for us, in His death, burial and resurrection. Then the Holy Spirit comes in with conviction of sin, and the need of the Saviour for that person. God draws that person into a personal relationship, bestows the free gift of salvation, and regeneration is the result. Ephesians 2:8,9 That is the greatest miracle, in that the repentant believing person is passed from spiritual death and bondage unto eternal life.

HEALING AND PRAYER

Many people have persisted in prayer for healing of a loved one or for themselves and have turned to the faith healer and been fooled. Don't they realize that God has a sovereign purpose for His doings, such as with the man born blind in the Gospels? John 9:1-3 It wasn't because of anybody's sin but for the glory of God. We don't always know God's will when we pray, so we should just keep on knocking and be surrendered to His infinite wisdom and his loving, sovereign will. (Matthew 7:7,8)

Others would argue that our prayers are not answered because we don't have enough faith. They are asking us to have faith in our faith, and they seem to miss that our faith is not in our faith, but in the person of our sovereign Lord. To ask in faith without being double minded is to be focused on God's will and be surrendered to it.

Others point us to James 5:13-16, where James gives a prescription for sin engendered sickness that has to be dealt with in order to have forgiveness and recovery. When confession has been made, not necessarily to the elders, but to our all knowing Lord, then they would be forgiven and the healing process begins. There is no indication that it will be accomplished without the use of the means of confession and receiving forgiveness. This example illustrates how some illnesses or physical symptoms can have spiritual roots.

CONCLUSION

I have no interest in or attraction to the healers, TV or otherwise, who claim to have a spiritual gift of healing and use it to make millions of dollars. Some of them have become multimillionaires at the expense of true gospel proclamation and discipling in the Christian life. God's people are givers and always have been. But their income and wealth is easily exploited by many who fail to test the spirits and see whether they be from God. It is a shame to see so much going into making multimillionaires of a few, rather than investing it in a good Gospel preaching church, or helping the poor, or a good missionary agency. I have great respect for true healers who use the appropriate means to produce healing and recovery. I appreciate the doctors and hospitals that have treated me over the years. I also have equal appreciation for all in the medical profession who use their skills and education for the treatment of all of our ills, especially three of my grandchildren who are ER nurses. God is at work healing through the use of all of these means.

I have not dealt with the phenomena of the Pentecostal movement's practice of "slain in the spirit," which is an exhaustive subject, and it has to do as much with audience hypnosis as healing, although a fake healing helps support their activities. I was invited to preach once at a "mourner's bench" church in Kentucky. The pastor-music leader was not satisfied with the audience response and suggested that on the next verse that they get with it. Sure enough, two ladies burst out with some kind of gibberish, and when the preaching of the Word followed, they sat glassy eyed through the sermon with no interest or response. They had already gotten what they came for. That was probably my first glimpse of audience hypnosis by an authority figure.

If you are one of those hungering Christians who does not have the gift of healing or tongues and you wonder about your spiritual standing because you don't, be comforted and look no further. Just covet the best gift of love and practice it in loving the Lord, the lost, and one another. I cannot believe that the Holy Spirit is pleased or honored in all things attributed to Him. Rejoice in God's sovereign bestowal of gifts, whatever they might be.

CHAPTER 16

Sacrament, Eucharist, Communion or Lord's Supper?

Various names have been used in church history to describe the simple memorial meal instituted by our Lord before His death. One of the most common is "Sacrament," which the dictionary defines as "any of certain rites ordained by Jesus and regarded as a means of grace." The Online Dictionary has much the same thought: "sacrament- a formal religious act conferring a specific grace on those who receive it." Closely related is the liturgical title "Eucharist," which describes "the consecrated bread and wine used in Holy Communion." Although Eucharist has the meaning of "thanksgiving," it should not be a preferred word to the Lord's Supper since it has its origin and practice in the corruption of biblical teachings. Another frequent description is "Communion" or "Holy Communion" depending on the practice of particular churches or denominations. This has been defined as "participation" or "a sharing in, or celebrating of, the Eucharist." The word "communion" in I Corinthians 11:16 is translated "participation," or "sharing" in other versions. These words are descriptive of the act of observance but not a name for the rite itself. All of these terms are closely related but raise questions about the true nature of the Lord's Supper.

At the center of the problem is the relationship of "grace" or "a means of grace." If this has reference to saving grace it contradicts grace which is the unmerited, undeserved gift of God. If it is descriptive of making a better person, it is hard to imagine what is in the mind of the participant and the person administering the rite. If grace is realized through self-examination and confession, that could make a sinning person a better person. No work of self-righteousness, or observance of religious ritual, can bring about saving grace.

The following research from various sources may help us to understand the nature of this problem:

This Holy Communion requires being "rightly disposed," to acquire an increase in "sanctifying grace," which is described as "the ability to take in the vision of God in the life to come," which may include "forgiveness of venial sin," an "increase in the virtue of love," to help the repentant keep from mortal sin. (*A Basic Catholic Catechism*) It is "essential for human salvation" helps to resist temptation and to avoid sin. (Catholic Web article) They "do not merely signify Divine grace...they cause that grace in the soul." (*Catholic Encyclopedia*) I guess all of these descriptions help them justify calling it "Holy Communion." It may be true that these teachings are shared by many Episcopalians.

The Lutheran teachings do not appear, to me, to be much better when they state "in the sacrament we receive forgiveness of sins... and salvation." They justify their teaching on the basis of the words, "shed for you for the remission of sin." (*Luther's Small Catechism*)

The Internet encyclopedia, *Wikipedia*, claims that "the followers of John Wesley, himself an Anglican clergyman, have typically affirmed that the sacrament of Holy Communion is an instrumental "Means of Grace."

The *Westminster Confession* asserts: "Sacraments are holy signs and seals of the covenant of grace." But it does reject the Catholic doctrine of transubstantiation. It calls it repugnant, "the cause of many superstitions and idolatries." It rejects the teaching that a priest can consecrate the elements in such a way as to transform them into the actual body and blood of the Lord.

The term "Lord's Supper" does not have all of these ideas associated with it. It is just a warm and familiar way to refer to the practice our Lord intended for His churches as a memorial of what He has done in His death on the cross for us. The *New Hampshire Confession of 1833* gives us a simple description of the practice as portrayed in the New Testament. Speaking of baptism and the Lord's Supper which are called "ordinances" in I Corinthians 11:2, 23, it asserts: "It is prerequisite to the privileges of a Church relation; and to the Lord's Supper, in which the members of the Church, by the sacred use of bread and wine, are to commemorate together the dying love of Christ"... It is the "Lord's Supper," or "the Lord's Table."

It is a sacred memorial, not a social meal and should always be treated with respect and reverence. The church is just the custodian of the ordinances. Too often, our culture governs our treatment of the Supper, rather than biblical teachings. Moses was given a pattern for building the Tabernacle and was admonished to stick with the pattern. (Hebrews 8:5) The Bible is still the all-sufficient rule of faith and practice. Our "pattern" for observing the Lord's Supper should come from His Word.

Baptists are not the only ones with some convictions about who should partake of the Supper and limits on participation. You will notice in their confession that baptism is a "prerequisite." And baptism assumes a previous acceptance of Christ as Saviour and confession of Him as such. Presbyterians have stated their position in article VIII of the Westminster Confession, where it asserts "all ignorant and ungodly persons...are unworthy of the Lord's table...or be admitted thereunto."

In 2002, the church-wide Holy Communion Study Committee of the Methodist Church concluded "That question is complicated by the tension between the implicit order of the sacraments - baptism preceding Holy Communion - and the United Methodist Church's unofficial but widely practiced 'open table.'"

Even the Anglican Bishop Ryle held to restrictions concerning its observance. He emphasized that it is not right to urge all professing Christians to partake at the Lord's Table. He urged that only the ones who have examined or are willing to examine themselves should partake. He further argued that it should only be those who have repented of known sin and resolved to lead a new life, for those who have a thankful remembrance of what Christ has done for us as symbolized in this ordinance. (*grace gems.org/Ryle*)

If you would examine closely the theology of other groups on this subject, I am sure you would find some qualifications for observing the rite in many other theological statements.

Conclusion: The simple message for us is the "Lord's Supper" is a memorial meal, instituted by our Lord to remember His sacrifice on the cross for us. It is trusting in His substitutionary death and confessing thereto. It is called the Lord's Supper in Scripture because He is the author of it. It was He who inaugurated it, and placed it in the church to be the guardian of all that it required until He comes again. The Lord's Supper is symbolically the heart of the Christian message.

CHAPTER 17

A Theology of Prayer

I am writing my thoughts on prayer because I have heard and seen too many building their whole theology of prayer upon one passage of Scripture. I will deal with that problem in this chapter. I do not try to exhaust all of the Scripture teaching on prayer or the particular passages that deal with prayer. I am selecting enough New Testament Scriptures to make my point - that you cannot build your theology of prayer on one passage or you will be disappointed many times with the results of your praying.

PRAYER EXHORTATIONS

There are many passages of Scripture that exhort us to pray. Perhaps I should begin with I Thessalonians 5:16: *"Pray without ceasing."* That certainly does not mean to assume a physical posture of kneeling, or even closing our eyes, but our relationship with God is such that we can bring every concern, large or small, to Him at any time. There is never a time in our Christian journey that we are not "standing in the need of prayer." And it is pleasing to our heavenly father to have us "tell Him all about our problems." In other places, Paul reinforces this exhortation as in Philippians 4:6, and in Ephesians 6:18, as he concludes his description of the Christian armor. He exhorts us to pray always *"with all prayer and supplication...in watching thereunto with all perseverance and supplication for all saints."*

Our Lord told His disciples to *"watch ye and pray, lest ye enter into temptation.* (Mark 14:38) We need that as much as they did. In Luke 18:1, He said, *"that men ought always to pray and not to faint."*

PRAYER HINDRANCES

There can be many hindrances to prayer, but I will mention just three here.

1. **A backslidden condition.** In Psalm 66:18, the psalmist affirms: *"If I regard iniquity in my heart, the Lord will not hear me."* James 5:16, 17 concluded that it was *"the effectual fervent prayer of a righteous man that availeth much."* He did not contend that we had to be perfect, as he illustrated with Elijah who was a man "of like passions." Even though he was a man of like passions, James considered him a "righteous man." Jesus Christ is our righteousness, but we are called to be a holy people. We need to deal with the problem of known sin if we are to be effective prayer warriors. We cannot condone it or look upon it with favor and expect God to look upon our requests with favor. Confession and the acceptance of forgiveness is the way to deal with the problem. Note also Isaiah's message in 59:1,2 - it was their "iniquities" that separated them from God, and as a result he promises (as God's messenger) that God would not hear them when they prayed.

2. **Wrong motives.** Again James (4:3) says: *"Ye ask, and receive not, because ye ask amiss, that ye may consume it upon your lusts."* It is proper to pray for legitimate needs but not for the luxuries we think we ought to have. A principle to be put into

practice here is: Is it for the glory of God? And am I willing to submit my will to God's?

3. **Lack of faith.** Again James advises us to ask in faith, without wavering, recognizing it is God's gift of wisdom that we need the most. Wavering is like the sea driven waves... *"Let not that man think that he shall receive anything of the Lord. A double minded man is unstable in all his ways."* (James 1:5-8) This describes a legitimate handicap or hindrance to prayer. But it is often used in a judgmental way to explain somebody else's lack of effectiveness, by insisting on having faith in your faith. The object of our faith is in an all-powerful, all-knowing, never changing sovereign God, not our faith in and of itself.

PRAYER'S PERSEVERANCE

When should we end our petitions? We have noted how Elijah prayed earnestly for three years and six months before the answer came. Many have prayed for decades for the salvation of a family member before the answer came. Jesus gave us some practical instructions in this regard: *"Ask, and it shall be given unto you; seek, and ye shall find; knock, and it shall be opened unto you."* (Luke 4:9,10) There are times when God is saying to us "keep on knocking." There are other times we need to be asking, "Is this petition for the glory of God?" Or God may want us to make some other examination of our petitions. There are also times that call for prayer <u>and fasting.</u> (Matt. 17:21) *"Howbeit this kind goeth not out but by prayer and fasting."*

PRAYER'S CONDITIONS

Some people are quick to jump on the promise of Matthew 18:19, where it is assured if two or three agree on a petition, it would be granted. This promise should not stand alone in your theology of prayer. Jesus also taught his followers to pray: *"Thy kingdom come. Thy will be done in earth, as it is in heaven."* (Matt. 6:10) I believe Jesus meant for us to share our concerns with others and to enlist them in intercessory prayer. But I don't believe that we should take the promise of Matthew 18:19 and "demand" that God honor it unconditionally. He is the Creator, we are the creature, and that means that we always bow to God's sovereignty, praying "not my will but thine be done." The all-encompassing condition of prayer is stated clearly in I John 5:14: *"If we ask anything according to his will, He heareth us."* Underline that - if we ask anything according to His will. God is not giving us a blank check to get everything we want. This verse qualifies what He will grant. Real prayer unites our thoughts and will with God's, and seeks His glory and our good. It recognizes and accepts the sovereignty of our awesome God. Jonathan Edwards held that "The Sovereignty of God is the stumbling block on which thousands fall and perish; and if we go contending with God about His sovereignty it will be our eternal ruin." Add to this another factor revealed in Romans 8:26, 27: *"Likewise the Spirit also helpeth our infirmities; for we know not what we should pray for as we ought; but the Spirit Himself maketh intercession for us with groanings which cannot be uttered.* Many prayers are selfish and foolish and we have learned by experience to be thankful that they were never answered. We often do not know what the will of the Lord is, but we know that it is perfect, that God is all-wise and His purpose for us is loving. He is working out His plan for our lives, when we pray "Not my will but thine be done." God is not heard by our much speaking or the use of a ministerial tone, liturgical formula, or ritual, but by our acquiescence to His will. The Holy Spirit, who dwells within us - our helper - takes our prayer to the Father through the work of His Son and makes it intelligible. To pray according to God's will is to welcome the teaching of His Spirit. He helps us understand what God' s doing in our lives. By that understanding we are comforted. The groanings, though indiscernible to us, are the instrument of the Spirit to mediate our petitions to the Father. The Spirit teaches us how to pray and what to pray for. If left to our natural inclinations, the petitions would be selfish.

Charles Haddon Spurgeon was not only a great preacher, but he was also a great man of prayer and he exhorted others to **"Let your thoughts be psalms, your prayers incense, and your breath praise."** Among his many messages on prayer are these warnings: to neglect prayer is to become barren, to neglect the reading of God's Word forfeits a fresh influence from on high. But the one who goes in secret to God with much diligence, and delights to mediate on God's message will have an overflowing heart; overflowing with love for God and others. "As his heart is, such will his life be." (*preceptaustin. org/spurgeongems_on_prayer.*)

CHAPTER 18

What is Close Communion?

By using this term, I am not conceding that "communion" is the proper New Testament term for the recurring ordinance. That is "The Lord's Supper." "Close Communion" is the term in common use in popular discussion and in variations of view-point or position. The common designations are "open-communion" or "close communion." "Open communion" may have some unspoken limitations such as not favoring unbelievers to participate. All terms using the word "communion" are historical-theological terms only. A survey of viewpoints reveal a variety of positions and definitions.

DEFINITIONS

Open, free, or mixed communion, "is, strictly speaking, that which permits any one who desires, and believes himself qualified, to come to the Lord's table, without any questions being asked, or conditions imposed, by the Church where the communion is observed." (Edward T. Hiscox, *The New Directory for Baptist Churches*)

Denominational communion is the practice of restricting the serving of the elements of communion to those who are members of a particular denomination, or sect. Though the meaning of the term varies slightly in different Christian theological traditions, it generally means a church or denomination limits participation either to members of their own denomination, or members of some specific class (e.g., baptized members of evangelical churches).

Full communion is a term used in Christian ecclesiology to describe relations between two distinct Christian communities or Churches that, while maintaining some separateness of identity, recognise each other as sharing the same communion and the same essential doctrines. (*Wikipedia*)

Restricted Communion is a term used by R. J. George to describe the theory which "invites to participation in the Lord's Supper all members in good standing in any of the evangelical Churches." It would exclude Unitarians, and Universalists.

Occasional Communion is the name George uses to describe "the theory that the Church may extend communion for a limited time, or in certain circumstances, to members of other denominations who are away from their own churches and providentially present at communion season. They may not agree with her profession, or desire to become members, but they desire the privileges of communion; or they "may claim to agree with her profession, but, owing to family relationships, or absence from her bounds, they are not in her fellowship, nor do they intend to be, but they wish to commune." (George, *Lectures on Pastoral Theology*)

To state the matter in simpler terms I would use just the terms "open-communion," "semi-close communion" or "denominational communion," and "close-communion" which recognizes some scriptural limitations on participating. Before making a case for any of these positions, it is interesting to note the various limitations practiced by mainline evangelical denominations. Do any of these besides the Baptists have a history of "close communion?"

Let us begin with the Presbyterians who are noted for orthodox reformed theology:

> The American Presbyterian Church holds to the doctrine of 'Close (near or intimate, not closed) Communion,' the Lord's Supper is to be administered to those who have been baptized and are of years and ability to examine themselves and are members of the church in good standing, either of the congregation which is observing the sacrament or of other congregations of the church. This standard of admission to the sacrament is commonly referred to as 'Close Communion.' (from *Lectures on Pastoral Theology* by R.J. George)

> (He also contends) that the Church is to have terms of communion; that they are to be strictly Scriptural; and that no one is to be admitted to communion except on these terms...There is no suggestion of non-essential truth in the Bible. The modern device is that only essential truth should be included in the terms of communion, and hence all who accept what are termed 'the essentials' should be admitted to communion. The distinction is without basis in the Word of God. In the structure of the human body, some members are more essential to life than others. It is easier to live without a hand than without a head. But a little finger is as really essential to a perfect human body as is the heart. There is also a body of divinity, and every portion of revealed truth is essential to the perfection of that body.

The Lutheran Church Missouri Synod has a stated position on the question: "The practice of close communion has been accepted as a practice flowing from the Scripture's teaching on church fellowship and unity in the Faith...the principle of close communion requires that only those who are in altar fellowship celebrate and partake... reception of Holy Communion not only implies but is a confession of the unity of faith."

The Episcopal standards and authorities are equally plain. *The Book of Common Prayer*, Order of Confirmation, declares: "There shall none be admitted to the holy communion, until such time as he be confirmed, or be ready and desirous to be confirmed...confirmation always coming after baptism."

Even the renowned Anglican Bishop Ryle held to further restrictions concerning its observance. He said that "It is not right to urge all professing Christians to go to the Lord's Table. There is such a thing as fitness and preparedness for the ordinance...The teaching of those who urge all their congregation to come to the Lord's Table, as if the coming must necessarily do every one good, is entirely without warrant of Scripture." He also held that a person must examine himself as to his fitness. That fitness included repentance, true faith and and a purpose to live a new changed life, and a thankful remembrance of Christ's death for him.

The historical Baptist position on close communion is a clearly stated position. It is expressed most famously in the *New Hampshire Confession of Faith*: "Christian Baptism is the immersion in water of a believer,....that it is prerequisite to the privileges of a Church relation; and to the Lord's Supper." It was always to be preceded by personal and solemn examination.

The statements of the respected Baptist theologian, Augustus Strong, are also clear. Professor Strong, in his *Systematic Theology*, says: "Since baptism is a command of Christ,....it follows that we cannot properly commune with the unbaptized...who perhaps unconsciously, violate the fundamental law of the Church." His reasoning is that disorderly walk disqualifies that person and destroys his right to the Lord's Supper.

THE CASE FOR OPEN COMMUNION

John G. Wenger, a Mennonite theologian, states the case for open communion without necessarily endorsing it in full. He deals with the matter of who should partake. He holds that, "Those who practice what is called open communion state that no believer of any persuasion should be excluded from the Lord's Supper because it is not a denominational table, it is the Lord's table." He felt that close communion would reflect on the piety of Christians in other denominations.

Hiscox gives a full rebuttal to these views and he is not hesitant to say:

> Open communion has but one argument to sustain it, viz., sympathy;...It has neither Scripture, logic, expediency, nor the concurrent practice of Christendom, either past or present, in its favor...To them, the Supper is rather a love-feast for Christian fellowship than a personal commemoration of Christ's love by those who have believed upon His name, and been baptized into the likeness of His death. But sympathy should not control in matters of faith, and in acts of conscience.

So also does A.H. Strong offer a rebuttal to the sentimental views of others, contending:

> Open communion must be justified, if at all, on one of four grounds: First, that baptism is not prerequisite to communion... Secondly, that Immersion on profession of faith is not essential to baptism... this is renouncing Baptist principles altogether. Thirdly,... if the conscience of the individual is to be the rule of the action of the church in regard to his admission to the Lord's Supper, why not also with regard to his

regeneration, his doctrinal belief, and his obedience to Christ's commands generally? Fourthly, that the church has no responsibility in regard to the qualifications of those who come to her communion.

This abandons the principle of the church's accountability to Christ. It also overthrows church discipline, which is also required in the Scriptures.

Strong also reasons that "Open communion logically leads to open church membership, and a church membership open to all, without reference to the qualifications required in Scripture,...would finally result in its actual extinction."

THE CASE FOR SEMI-CLOSE OR DENOMINATIONAL COMMUNION

Granted that the scripture alone should be our guide in all matters of faith and practice and should define the limits of participation at the Lord's Table as well, this is the only occasion for the practice of what has been called "inter-church communion" or "denominational communion" or "semi-close communion." The Scripture account is given in Acts 20:4-8 where the Lord's Supper was administered by the church at Troas. The context shows that visiting brethren participated. It was the practice of the church to administer the Supper that only the members of the church had that right to participate. But since the visiting brethren were of like faith and order, it was allowed. B. H. Carroll explains this unusual occasion in his book, *An Interpretation of the English Bible*, Vol.12, (p. 363).

At this point in the history of Christianity, there were only New Testament churches. There were no distinguishing labels of separate and contrary beliefs. They were just a body of baptized believers and probably without any formal membership rolls. They were of "like faith and order" until heretical ideas caused the multiple divisions we have today. So this instance should be understood in this light.

THE CASE FOR CLOSE OR CHURCH-COMMUNION

The case for this practice, for the Baptist, is supported by the clear statement of the New Hampshire Confession of Faith, which requires "the immersion of a believer" as a "prerequisite to the privileges of a church relation and to the Lord's Supper, in which the members of the church are to commemorate together the dying love of Christ, preceded always by solemn self-examination." It is also supported by the statements already quoted from the Baptist theologian, A.H. Strong. But more than this, it is supported by the following scriptural support:

1. The divine order of Acts 2:41,42: "Then they that gladly received his words were baptized; and the same day there were added unto them about three thousand souls, and they continued steadfastly in the apostle's doctrine (teaching) and fellowship and in breaking of bread and prayers." The expression "breaking of bread" may designate an ordinary meal as it does in Acts 20:11, Luke 24:35, and as it most likely does in Acts 2:46. In this latter verse, the expression is connected to the act of "eating their meat," and most naturally suggests the act of sharing common food for a meal. But in Acts 2:42, it is most natural that this act describes the act mentioned in Acts 20:7 and in I Corinthians 10:16. This participation is only symbolic of our continued appropriation of Christ by faith. The Scripture clearly suggests a divine order - (1) Responding to the Gospel, (2) Baptism into a church fellowship, and (3) Observing the supper with that fellowship.

2. Paul's statement that it is impossible to observe the Lord's Supper when there are divisions in the congregation (I Corinthians 11:17-21) can only have meaning and significance in a situation where the members are logically the ones participating. To insist on the participation of people who are not of like faith and order is only to invite and enlarge

division. The problem of divisions can only be dealt with inside the local congregation. The church cannot discipline those outside its membership. The Corinthian church had the responsibility of correcting a scandalous situation before they could actually "eat the Lord's Supper." Until they did, it was just pretense. "This is not to eat the Lord's Supper." *(Authorized Version).* "It is impossible to eat the Lord's Supper." *(American Standard Version)*

3. Paul's command to discipline the immoral persons include cutting them off from the privileges of the Lord's Supper - "with such an one, no not to eat." (I Cor. 5:11) Paul makes it plain that this action has to be limited to "them that are within." God judges those on the outside but the church (here the church at Corinth) has the responsibility within, "Therefore put away from yourselves that wicked person." (I Cor. 5:13) The church has no control or power of discipline over the person outside its own membership. The implication is obvious - only those who were subject to discipline could properly partake of the Supper. This is not to deny the necessity of self-examination which is another matter entirely.

4. The symbolism of the one loaf is limited to the particular church participating. (I Cor. 10:17) The one loaf mentioned here is not only symbolic of the one offering for sin, but also the unity of the body partaking of the Supper - "For we many are one loaf, one body; for we are all partakers from that one loaf." Or, as the *Revised Standard Version* puts it, "Because there is one loaf, we who are many are one body, for we all partake of the same loaf." Obviously, their practice was to observe the Supper with one loaf, and I presume as the people broke off a piece of the bread, it symbolized their constant dependence on the work of Atonement finished by Jesus, and their recognition of the perpetual need of Him as Saviour.

THE CASE FOR CLOSE BAPTISM

The problem of "close communion" has not so much to do with the Supper as it does with baptism. Most of the historic denominations recognize in some way that baptism precedes the recurring practice of partaking of the Lord's Supper. The real issue focuses on the validity of baptism by sprinkling or some other substitute for immersion of the believer. "But inasmuch as they hold that sprinkling as well as immersion is baptism, their communion is more open, and that of Baptists is more close, by the difference between their views of baptism and ours, and by that difference only." (Hiscox)

Miles Bullock, a Methodist divine, says that "Close communion, as it is generally termed, is the only logical and consistent course for Baptist churches to pursue. If their premises are right, their conclusion is surely just as it should be." And he commends the firmness of Baptists in not inviting to the communion those whom they regard as unbaptized. He says: "They do not feel willing to countenance such laxity in Christian discipline. Let us honor them for their steadfastness in maintaining what they believe to be a Bible precept, rather than criticize and censure because they differ with us concerning the intent and mode of Christian baptism, and believe it to be an irrepealable condition of coming to the Lord's table." (*What Christians Believe*, p.103, 4) This conclusion is in agreement with Dr. Strong who held that "The obligation to commune is no more binding than the obligation to profess faith by being baptized. Open communion, however, treats baptism as if it were optional, while it insists upon communion as indispensable."

CONCLUSION

Since the reality does not correspond to the historical and biblical support for "close communion, and church discipline is rarely practiced, how do we account for the reality of a widely practiced "open communion?" We have a heard a lot about "dumbing down" in the educational arena. There has also been a pretty thorough "dumbing down" of the appreciation and meaning of the ordinances of baptism and the Lord's Supper in ecclesiastical circles. It has even been taken out of the church as a church ordinance and made a social religious nicety in informal fellowship circles. Three powerful influences may account for it. They are ecumenicalism, interdenominationalism, and sentimentalism. Seeking the lowest common denominator in order to achieve unity and numbers may be a practical tool, but it is not honoring to the sacred Scriptures. Those governed by sentiment or sympathy will look upon church communion as narrow. Again Strong has an appropriate answer: "The choir is not narrow because it does not include those who can only make discords, nor is the sheep fold intolerant that refuses to include wolves, nor the medical society that excludes quacks, nor the church that does not invite the disobedient and schismatic to its communion."

How then are we to deal with shallow reality? Does the church have any more responsibility than to teach the Scriptures on the subject? They certainly have that responsibility in the Great Commission. But as to inviting, remember it is the Lord's Table. "It is the Lord's table, and not ours; therefore we have no right to invite any but such as the Lord has designated. If it were our table we could invite whomsoever we would. As it is, we must obey the Lord at His own table." (Hiscox) The least the church can do is post in the church bulletin, or display on a screen, the words of Acts 4:41, 42, and the part of their confession that affirms what we believe about the participation.

But going beyond that, as to "barring" or "prohibiting," it doesn't work in church growth situations. Many worshipers act upon their own sentiments and nothing else matters. They will participate anyway. "Policing" the table can detract from the worship experience to the extent that the unity is lost and a spirit of legalism would prevail. At that point "close communion" really does become "closed communion." Let other denominations, that are not of like faith and order as ours, practice their creeds and disciplines and let us render them respect, and honor their worship and practices by not violating their intentions or creeds. We do not have to participate in those situations, nor is it proper. If New Testament faith is followed by New Testament baptism on the part of every believer, every Christian would be a member of a New Testament church and would thus have a place where he could repeatedly and properly observe the Lord's Supper and preserve the unity and discipline of the body participating.

CHAPTER 19

Church Discipline- Where Is It?

IN THE ROMAN CHURCH

Discipline, is considered man-made and can be changed by the church at any time and as often they wish to do so. They justify this upon the basis of their authority to "bind and loose." (Matthew 18:18) They emphasize that this authority extends beyond, as well as includes church discipline.

IN PROTESTANTISM

Lutheran

To understand fully the practice of Lutherans in church discipline, I suppose we would have to know the position of each synod. We can learn something from the example and statements of the Concordia Lutheran Conference. I rather doubt, though, that there is consensus among the Lutherans. To promote our understanding of their practice,

I shall use their statement anyway, with all due respect for their loyalty to the Scriptures.

> "In the **narrower** sense it means the dealing carried on in a local congregation with a member according to the Word of God, with reference to a particular sin, for the purpose of leading that member to repentance, or if this fails, of excommunicating him from its fellowship. It is the order by which the local congregation testifies that a manifest and impenitent sinner no longer stands in fellowship with the Church of Christ. II Corinthians 6:14." *(Concordia Lutheran Conference Website)*

The Lutherans are to be commended for relying on several Scriptural accounts, to justify their position. One is the reference to Revelation 2:2, where the congregation at Ephesus is praised because it did not allow evil ones in its fellowship. Another occasion was the account in Revelation 2:14, 15, 20, where the congregation at Pergamos is reprimanded because it did not exercise discipline on false teachers and such as lead ungodly lives. In 1 Timothy 1:20, Paul excluded two men on the authority of the congregation from the church. On still another occasion, in I Timothy 5:20, in a case of public offense, discipline was to be exercised before the whole congregation.

We are reminded also in I Corinthians 5:1-13, where Paul emphasizes the importance of discipline before proceeding with the Lord's Supper. Other Scriptures mentioned are Romans 16:17, 2 Corinthians 2:6, 2 Thessalonians 3:6, 14, 15, and 2 John 10 and 11. At least in this above website, they conclude that a true Lutheran Congregation practices church discipline. Again, I say the Lutherans are to be commended. (See the *Concordia Lutheran Website*)

Reformed

These statements from the Westminster Confession express the views and policies of Presbyterians and other Reformed groups: "Church censures are necessary for the reclaiming and gaining of offending brethren; for deterring of others from like offenses; for purging out of that leaven...for vindicating the honor of Christ, and the holy profession of the gospel..." It goes on to discuss further the reasons and prescribe the responsibility of church officers in light of these truths, from the nature of the offense, ending in excommunication for some whose case is of an extreme nature. They go as far as to list these offenses and how to deal with them. The only list that I could give you would simply be the Scripture references that deal with that subject. Nevertheless, I am impressed by the way the Reformed have adopted a position, and spelled it out. That portrays the possession of deep conviction. Again, I commend and respect them the same as the Lutherans in their concern.

Baptist

I know of know no definitive document from the Southern Baptist Convention that deals with church discipline. The only thing that comes close is a book first published in 1962 by Broadman Press: *Baptist Church Discipline.* Since Southern Baptists, the largest denomination of Baptists in our country, seem to have no urgent interest concerning maintaining a regenerate membership and how to practice such discipline, I think the criticism of pastors is warranted. I have been a Southern Baptist for most of my life and have observed the practice of discipline in many churches. Southern Baptists are not adverse to self criticism. It has often been remarked that "we are many, but not much." Many seem unwilling to do anything about it. Our numbers grow, but not the quality of our doctrine, or our manner of living. I think I may be qualified to offer some self criticism of my chosen denomination.

The churches in our denomination do have its share of respected Christian leaders like Billy Graham, and Al Mohler; Tony Dungy and Tim Tebow in the sports world; Mike Huckabee in the political and broadcasting world, and many other godly men and leaders in their field. We are grateful for their testimony and manner of life. On the other hand, we have the opposite opinion of some because their manner of life does not fit the Christian profession, even though they have professed faith and been baptized. For them, we have to apologize.

Where are the roots to his problem? It did not happen overnight. It did not sneak up on us. I would offer an answer with regret, that our churches have not nurtured the new believer. Often the only testimony they can offer is they walked down the aisle to make their profession, and were baptized. This also exposes a lack of counseling on the part of the church, to examine them to make sure they understand the way to be saved, and they have actually experienced repentance and faith.

When a new believer is converted, it is the responsibility of the pastor and church to shepherd that individual. Our work doesn't stop with admission to the fellowship, as important as that is; they are a blessing to us, and we should be a blessing to them by declaring the whole counsel of God. We should lovingly lead them to a genuine, knowledgeable, learned acceptance of the great doctrines of the Christian faith and an honorable way of living as Christ's disciple. We must never overlook that they are in different stages of Christian growth.

In light of this, the criticism is justified when they say we have "dipped them and dropped them." That is the result of our obsession with numbers. This produces shallow Christians in shallow churches. This is a criticism which should always be avoided.

Now that it is obvious we have not practiced church discipline as commanded in the New Testament, we look for the human reasons or excuses. It is false and hypocritical to assert that we love them too much to discipline them. Often this is the method to lead them in a more abundant life. Do you treasure their mediocrity more?

There are other human reasons for avoiding church discipline. They are not concerned for the purity of the church, which explains their neglect. I have never met a preacher that denied the fact that the Scriptures teach church discipline. Yet they are content to protect someone's feelings. When we get overly concerned for feelings, we hamper the work of the Holy Spirit to convict, to instruct, and to guide into all truth.

Other people besides the minister are involved in maintaining a meaningless membership. They do not want their friend or relative removed from the roll. It is difficult enough to remove those persons that are deceased and impossible to locate. If a local member, they have an obligation to support the church with their time and money. Failure to do so over a long period of time is good grounds for removing them from the church roll. Some denominations to not have church rolls. That obscures and hinders any effort to disciple them.

There have been some efforts to deal with these problems in our history. Of some note, is the adoption of a church covenant, where the individual baptized believer pledges certain things to the whole body. The covenant was not a legalistic tool to force conformity, but to pledge, to endeavor to reach the goals set forth. I regret to say that it has been sadly ignored in recent years. For some churches, it has been watered down in order to escape a pledge to abstain from alcoholic beverages.

When I accepted a call to one church, I led an evangelistic team to visit first the inactive members we could find, to see what they understood about their Christian profession. It is sad to report that half of them did not have assurance of salvation and probably had not been saved.

Other Baptist groups may not be so lax in church discipline. They might be overbearing or inconsistent in their practice, but at least they have a concern for purity in the church. There is a caution regarding being too severe. Church discipline should always be grounded in a redemptive purpose for the action required, which is Christian growth and the unity of believers.

PART III

DIFFICULT ESCHATOLOGY
(END TIME EVENTS)

CHAPTER 20

When Will Jesus Come?

I did not entitle this chapter "When will Jesus come again?" because I wanted to affirm first to anyone chancing to read this that the Messiah has come, and His name is Jesus. He was born of a virgin. He lived among sinful men without ever committing sin. He has finished His redemptive work on the cross. He was crucified and buried in a borrowed tomb. Death could not keep its prey. He arose from the dead, appeared to more than 500 witnesses, and ascended into heaven. Those that watched Him disappear into the clouds were assured by the angels that he would come again. "Ye men of Galilee, why stand ye gazing up into heaven? This same Jesus, which is taken up from you into heaven, shall so come in like manner as ye have seen him go into heaven." (Acts 1:9-11) When Jesus was preparing his disciples to face his death, he told them "I go to prepare a place for you. And if I go and prepare a place for you, I will come again and receive you unto myself; that where I am, there ye may be also." (John 14:2, 3)

Since the time of His ascension the writers of the Holy Scriptures have held up the promise of His return, and showed us how to live in the meantime: "Denying ungodliness and worldly lusts, we should live soberly, righteously, and godly, in this present world; looking for that blessed hope, and the glorious appearing of the great God and our Saviour Jesus Christ." (Titus 2:12,13) The "blessed hope" was very real and precious to the early Christians, as it should be to us today. Because of that, many people have tried to answer the question: "When will Jesus come again?"

Some have said the return of Christ is imminent. By this they do not mean immediate. By this they mean that it may or may not be in the future, but it could occur at any moment. There is no prophetic event that has not already occurred to prevent the event happening at any time. That would be consistent with the coming being a "blessed hope." There is one big problem with that hope for some, since the Anti-Christ has not been revealed, the temple has not been rebuilt, and Armageddon has not taken place. I do not share those beliefs, so I can affirm the second coming event without depending on those events occurring.

Some have said they knew the exact time and year, despite the fact that Jesus said, " But of that day and hour, no man, no, not the angels of heaven, but my father only." (Matt. 24:36) One of the most famous illustrations of this was William Miller who made careful calculations from prophecy and other resources and said that the year would be 1844. The day was determined to be October 22. Many of his followers sold their homes and left their employment to proclaim their message and await the return. Well, it did not happen and approximately 100,000 of his followers were greatly disappointed. You would think this would be a powerful lesson and there would be no repeat of time setting. Alas, that was not the case, for many since that time have done the same thing, and when it doesn't happen, they do not even seem to be embarrassed.

I pastored a church in an area where there was a "Truelight Church." It was well known in the community that they had a set such a day and did their preparations, but He did not come. You have cause to wonder what happened to their estates and how they recovered to go on with life.

Some have said He would return after the temple in Jerusalem is rebuilt, as Ezekiel prophesied, and the Anti-Christ is revealed. With their charts and proof-texts they can dogmatically portray all the events of prophecy. If that is true, then He cannot return at any time, since those events have not occurred. Then "The Blessed Hope" is diminished. It appears that the early Christians held out the hope that the event could happen even in their own day. Peter recognized that there were scoffers regarding the Lord's return who were saying, "Where is the promise of his coming? For since the fathers fell asleep, all things continue as they were from the beginning of the creation." (II Peter 3:4)

Some have said that He has already come, in ridiculous substitutes such as "in like manner as ye have seen him go." They equate this with progress in humanitarian enterprises is not the second coming. You can point to the hospitals, orphanages, homes for the aged, and schools. They are the outgrowth of Christian works, but not His personal return. Death is not the "second coming." When the Christian is dying, he can truthfully say, "the Lord has come for me," but that is not the second coming. After his coming, there will be no more death which we may regard here as our worst enemy. The advent of the Holy Spirit in Acts 2 is not the second coming. I am told there are as many as 150 references after the advent of the Holy Spirit that refer to the second coming. I admit that I have not counted them, but I am aware of such a significant number that this explanation should easily be discarded. The second coming will be personal, bodily, and visible.

Some have said he will come before "the Great Tribulation." Some have said that it would be in the middle of that period. Others have said that it will come after that period. Some have made the second coming a second and third coming with their dispensational theology of a "secret rapture" and a "revelation." His promise to "come again" did not spell out phases of His return but the fact of it.

I have not tried to give an answer to the question. His coming again is still my blessed hope. I am content to leave that to the heavenly father. I accept the assurance of Peter: "But the day of the Lord will come as a thief in the night; in which the heavens shall pass away with a great noise, and the elements shall melt with fervent heat, the earth and the works that are therein shall be burned up." (II Peter 3:10) Now it is time to visit William Miller again. I am told that the words on his gravestone were to the effect: "At the appointed time the Lord will come." That appointed time is His time, not ours. Perhaps, if his zeal for time setting had not been so acute, the Millerite movement would not have given rise to Seventh Day Adventism, Jehovah's Witnesses, and Bahai. Miller's final resignation was a biblical one, and in accord with the great creeds and confessions of Christendom.

The last great promise in Revelation from our Lord was: "Behold, I come quickly." He repeats it three times. (Rev. 22:7, 12, 20) The proclamation also included the news: "My reward is with me to give every man according as his work shall be." The closing plea of the apocalypse was: "Even so, come, Lord Jesus." Is that your desire? I remember reading about a minister in an almost impossible situation as the pastor of a backslidden, fussing congregation. All he could think of was: "Come, Lord Jesus, come." Shortly thereafter he was called to pastor a different group in a lovely community, where they loved one another; they loved him and his family, and took Jesus rather seriously. He found himself praying: "Come, Lord Jesus, but not just now!" I'm afraid there are many Christian people who are so comfortable, and so in love with the world that they can only pray: "Come, Lord Jesus, but not yet!"

We are brought back to the simple affirmation of our Lord - "I will come again." A story is told of an incident in Spurgeon's family. The great Charles H. Spurgeon once left home with his promise that he would return some day during the following week. On Monday, the little children were full of joyful expectation. "Father may come today," they told each other happily. They helped tidy up the house. They kept their clothing neat and clean, for they said "perhaps he will come today." Failure to look for him on Monday would have revealed a lack of confidence in his promise. Tuesday, Wednesday, Thursday, Friday, and Saturday came. They were confident that he would return at some hour in the day and they kept doing the same. They were jubilant with anticipation. At some hour of this day they were sure He would return. And on Saturday he came. Mrs. Spurgeon advised him: "When you go away again, do not tell us exactly when you will return. The children have never been so helpful and well-behaved as when they were looking each day for your coming."

There are some valuable lessons to learn from this incident. Jesus hasn't told us when He will return so as to forearm us against setting dates. The day of His return is His day. He will keep His promise. We can be faithfully looking for Him. After all, that is our blessed hope. We can and should keep our lives clean, as though He could return at any moment. We may be in the Saturday of the age. ARE YOU READY?

CHAPTER 21

Who or What Will Destroy the Planet?

There are many strident voices today that sound their alarms, predict a coming destruction of our planet and assign blame to man's activities. Their battle cry is "save the planet!" Their solution is more and more government regulation that can have an adverse effect upon our society and more especially the poor. Wealthy elitists, who always claim to know best, love to quote selected scientists in support of their positions. They would love to force their views upon all humanity. That there is coming an end to history should not be disputed. However, man, created in the image of God and assigned a stewardship responsibility for the care of the earth, will not be the agent that destroys the planet. It will do us well to consider the so-called scientific threats and respond in a responsible manner.

OVERPOPULATION

One of the more subdued cries is from the alarmists that claim our planet cannot sustain the increase in population trends. They then claimed that all humans and even living things are threatened because their will not be enough food supply. They claim that our actions in every sphere of life will contribute to this result. Plowing up more land, and destroying forests which are the habitat for wild animals, are destructive forces. Population growth continuing will require more food, and more growth acres. They say this, ignoring the fact that our farmers are able to produce more food per acre with the appropriate fertilizer. Soon, they argue, we will not be able to provide it. The forests that provide the lumber and other materials to build our houses will no longer be available. They claim this in despite the fact that the forests renew themselves, the wild life adapt to human occupation and even mix with us. Some are destructive of our gardens and crops. Others are a delight to behold. When they mix, they are protected from destruction. These wealthy elitists seem to have nothing better to do than to conceive and promote their solution to the changes in human activity, which they claim is the only way to save the planet even though they do not live by their own beliefs. Please, leave us alone. We can do it better than you think, and our solutions are better.

On the opposite side of the picture, ponder what could be done by empowering the masses to develop more farm land in order to provide the food needed for their communities to treat malnutrition and prevent starvation.

Isn't it amazing how people who have a Christian worldview deal with this problem? It's great to have an awesome God! We send missionary farmers to people in order to help them know how to grow their gardens in and provide the different vegetables for a healthy diet. They could encourage local entrepreneurs to go into farming in a big way, whose benefits then profit other communities around them. A godless, secular world view cannot match this solution.

In rebuttal, consider the evidence arguments presented by Steve Mosher. He points out several facts relevant to the discussion. He doesn't entertain ideas such as the one child policy of China. That has already exposed many worse problems and the cruelty of a controlled society. Here are the facts that are ignored in this debate:

1. The birth rate has decreased globally in wealthy countries and in several third world countries.
2. The fertility rate from the 1950's has fallen from 2.8 to 1.6 in the world's most advanced countries, and in the third world countries it has fallen from 6.0 to 3.0 per woman. This dated from the 1960's. Imagine what it would be in 2014.
3. With present birth rate figures, it is anticipated that "the world population will stabilize around 2050 on about 8 – 10 billion according to demographic experts."
4. It is not justified to prognosticate a population explosion because much is not known about deaths from diseases and natural calamities. The news seems to be reporting almost every day hundreds of deaths from ruthless slaughterings from tribal groups in the Middle East and Africa. The toll from earthquakes and floods is also great.
5. The population is not facing explosion, but implosion, as the fertility rate drops in other countries. "This is why *The New York Times* has called overpopulation 'one of the myths of the Twentieth Century.'" (Steve Mosher, *Population Control*)

GLOBAL WARMING

Climate change is not the same as "global warming." When the global warming term became untenable, environmentalists switched to "climate change." As far as we know, there have always been periodic variations in the temperature of the earth, and there always will be variations from warming to cooling. These may be caused by "sunspots," ocean currents, or some other creative act of God in nature. The global warming hoax is an alarmist's position assigning the blame to man's use of fossil fuels. It is the position of environmental religion. Because of it, they have a way of attacking the petroleum and nuclear power industries with little regard for its effect upon world economies and the poor, both in the United States and third world developing countries. The ill-advised use of grains for bio-fuel has already had a tremendous impact on the world's poor.

The foolish attempt to curtail supply and demand for oil already has had a devastating effect on our economy. My own personal conviction is that God knew we would have need of these resources; He put them there for our use; He has given us the wisdom and technology to extract them in a sensible way. I know that the secular fundamentalists will hoot, snicker and sneer at that affirmation, since their worldview has already ruled out the existence and role of the creator. But they do not have a better solution to the world's problems. My convictions on this matter stem from my Christian worldview and belief in the providence of a sovereign, omnipotent, all-knowing, creator God who sustains the universe He made. If we ruled out the use of carbon emissions, we would still have need for oil in powering millions of automobiles, buses, planes and trains around the world that are a long way from being obsolete. We rely on hundreds of petroleum-based products in our daily lives, including plastics, clothing, disposable diapers, medicines, appliances, shoes, toys, computers, cars, and building materials to name a few. When oil has been depleted, God will have provided other materials in the planet, the technological wisdom for the discovery, and production to meet man's needs. I am confident of this outcome until our Lord returns and history (His Story) will be ended.

I am never overly impressed with the claims of scientists in matters as important as this one is to our world, when I consider their support for the evolutionary theory of Charles Darwin, which is an equal hoax. There are many other cases, though not as important as these two, where scientists have been proven wrong. Their theories were not based on fact. Fortunately, there has been, and still are, many scientists who are not caught in the secular, anti-god trap.

There is no scientific consensus for man-made global warming as the media and radical environmentalists would have us believe. There is a lot of conflicting evidence as well as respected scientists and scholars who disagree. The Cornwall Alliance and Acton Institute has published a reasonable treatment of the whole problem in *Environmental Stewardship in the Judeo-Christian Tradition.* I am listing some pertinent points the Cornwall Alliance has presented. I wish I could go into more detail, but you can learn better by going to their publication. Here is only a summary of their conclusions:

1. Proper environmental stewardship puts human needs first when there are other needs in conflict with that need.
2. Carbon Dioxide is essential to plant growth and better productivity. Studies have shown that doubling the amount of CO_2 in the atmosphere has resulted in a 35% growth in productivity. That could only effect the capitalist, but would be an indirect boon for the world's poor.
3. This increase in CO_2 helps us all to feed the world's poor. That pleases our Lord who admonished us to care for the poor, because they are always with us.
4. The efficiency of plant growth will be more production in warmer and wetter climates, and lower altitudes. That conclusion is reasonable.
5. Due to political activists and other like factors, scientists abandoned facts, reason and logic in the 1980's. When it has taken root in the thinking of the populace, it has been hard to correct. Note how much destruction has occurred due to pseudo science. It has resulted in destroying our economy, and made us captive to countries who have found it in their best interest to capitalize on our foolish decisions. We have had to do it in order to meet the great needs of our people, or face a rebellion in the populace. Modern environmentalism is the culprit destroying out freedoms, because it is anti-human, it is against economic development, and, it is anti- reason. I have felt free to add my own comments when I was convinced they were not in conflict with the positions stated.

Thomas Gale Moore, in his book *Climate of Fear,* gives us much the same reasons why we should reverse the actions of government policies that favor the modern environmentalist movement. It is a movement, a crusading movement favoring the secular controlled society. He does make some additional points that help us understand the whole issue and why we should steadfastly resist this dangerous movement.

1. One reason is his conviction that good stewardship celebrates human life, freedom, and economic development. These are compatible and essential for the good of the whole environment. (p. 109)
2. In 1997, a petition was offered and published by the Oregon Institute of Science and Medicine that urged the rejection of the Kyoto protocol similar proposals. Among their reasons was it would not benefit the health and welfare of all.
3. There is no convincing evidence that greenhouse gases will increase global warming and disrupt the earth's climate. This is not a reality now and never will be. (p. 96)
4. "In many developing countries, the basics of sufficient and pure water and food, along with clothing, shelter, transportation, health care, communication...still remain elusive for many people." It is wrong for the people in developed countries to impose their own environmental beliefs on people who are still struggling to survive. (p. 68)
5. Frederic Seitz, past president of the National Academy of Sciences, represented over seventeen thousand scientists opposed the Kyota treaty on the basis of flawed ideas. They maintained that the increase of hydrocarbon was helpful, not harmful, and the treaty would only have a negative effect. (p. 93)
6. Global warming would quite likely improve the quality of human health as well. For further study, please refer to the book by Moore: (Thomas Gale Moore, *Climate of Fear: Why We Shouldn't Worry about Global Warming,* p.91, 92)

Vaclav Klaus maintains that **"the largest threat to freedom, democracy, the market economy, and prosperity at the end of the 20th and at the beginning of the 21st century is no longer socialism...It is, instead, the ambitious, arrogant, unscrupulous**

ideology of environmentalism." (Vaclav Klaus, *Blue Planet in Green Shackles*)

In spite of all this evidence to the contrary, environmental politicians declare that the debate is closed by consensus. How foolish can you get?

NUCLEAR WARFARE

For relevance to this discussion, I will simply use the definition and discussion of Wikipedia to describe this theory:

> "It is one of the alarmist's fears by those people who are opposed to nuclear defense weapons and our energy facilities to define nuclear warfare as the term usually used for confrontations betwen opposition forces which would result in mutual destruction. They claim that it would have a long range damaging effect on people and plant growth that would last for decades and even millennia. They claim that without regard to the recovery of the Japanese cities that were bombed in World War II."

Others have called limited nuclear war "global nuclear holocaust in slow motion," arguing that once such a war took place, others would be sure to follow over a period of decades, effectively rendering the planet uninhabitable in the same way that a "full-scale nuclear war" between superpowers would, only taking a much longer and more agonizing path to achieve the same result.

It is true that a nuclear war would exert great destructive force upon the planet, but we do not know to what extent and we hope it will never happen. The extent of destruction would only be speculative. We have a more sure word of prophecy and authority concerning the end of our planet as we know it. We have only to turn to our next agent.

THE OMNIPOTENT GOD

"But the day of the Lord will come as a thief in the night; in the which the heavens shall melt with fervent heat, the earth also and the works that are therein shall be burned up. Seeing then that all these things shall be dissolved, what manner of persons ought ye to be in all holy conversation and godliness, looking for and hasting unto the coming of God, wherein the heavens being on fire shall be dissolved, and the elements shall melt with fervent heat? Nevertheless we, according to his promise, look for new heavens and a new earth, wherein dwelleth righteousness." (II Peter 3:10-13)

It should be obvious with only a superficial exposition of this passage, that the Almighty God, in His time and in His way, will author the great general conflagration of the planet. Many have debated whether this has reference to a renewing process or a replacement creation. For our discussion, it is enough to describe the destruction of our planet and it makes clear that God does it suddenly and purposefully. It will include not only our planet but the heavenly bodies. John Wesley states his insight when he suggests: "And has not God already provided for this...by the stores of subterranean fire which are so frequently bursting out" in the volcanoes of the earth?" He also envisions the inclusiveness of the action which includes the earth "and the works thereof" which are identified as nature and art as well as the earth itself.

CONCLUSION

For the overpopulation alarmist, too many people make the planet incapable of supporting human life. Their key word is "unsustainable." So they advocate support for planned parenthood, government edicts as to size of the family, etc., while the evidence does not support any alarm. For the global warming adherents, the key words are "save the planet" by controlling climate change. Who do they think they are? God, and only God, can control the climate. He always has and

He always will. I see no evidence from the various computer models that man is responsible for climate changes, nor can he manage it. It is in God's hands. The popular spiritual expresses it so well: "He's got the whole world in His hands…He's got the wind and the rain in His hands…He's got the sun and the moon in His hands." For the nuclear warfare believer, the danger for the planet is that it becomes "uninhabitable" but it still exists. When we turn to the Word of God we learn what is really going to happen to the planet in God's time and in His omnipotent way. Our concern now should be just as much for moral pollution and the provision for man's basic needs in a civilized world. Demonizing the petroleum or pharmaceutical industries isn't going to solve any of our problems. Our greatest concern ought to be our eternal destiny. Jesus said: "I am the Way." He died in our place. Trust Him as Saviour and receive His forgiveness and acceptance as a child of God forever, with the assurance of heaven as your eternal home. (Acts 16:31)

CHAPTER 22

What is Heaven Like?

I imagine that most people get their understanding of the nature of heaven from either John 14 or Revelation 21. I would like to begin at a different place. The passage that strikes me as the most enlightening is I Corinthians 2:9, "But as it is written, Eye hath not seen, nor ear heard, neither have entered into the heart of man, the things God hath prepared for them that love him." The passage in John 14 is sketchy yet assuring and comforting. The passage in Revelation is highly symbolic and intriguing. The passage in Corinthians is mysterious but all encompassing.

From the beginning of our thoughts on this subject, we must affirm that everybody that talks about heaven isn't going there. For some it is a grand wish of "if," not "when," we get to heaven. It is also true that everybody's concept is not a good one. It is not based solidly on a biblical foundation, and they do not have the right priorities in their thinking.

In John 14, Jesus spoke of "preparing" a place for His followers. The "mansions" or "dwelling place" impresses us as very desirable and attractive since it is through toil, and sweat, and financial assets we are able to acquire a temporary dwelling place here. And the place Jesus described would be for eternity, whereas our homes here become obsolete and we desire something better. The main message of this passage was not to give a full description of heaven but to comfort and assure His disciples that what He had to do was "to obtain for you a right to be there, and to possess your 'place.'" (Jamison, Fausset and Brown) The many mansions assured them there was a place for each and room for all. The promise suggests a sufficiency in space to accommodate all of those believers He was gathering to witness His glory, and enjoy fellowship with Him throughout the endless ages.

When we come to the passages in Revelation we have to understand first the nature of Revelation. In Revelation 1:1, the writer signifies and certifies the his use of symbols to give his message. In every scene in this cosmic drama, he employs symbols to convey truth to his believing listeners. In times of persecution, it was necessary to hide truths from the persecutors and unveil them to those familiar with the significance of the symbols. So he uses historical places, numbers and objects to fit his literary style and message. But the basic rule of interpretation is that Revelation is a book of symbols as the writer declares.

When we come to Revelation 21, we are introduced to the New Jerusalem, which is the people of God gathered through the ages in that glorious place. Forget for the moment the beauty described in earthly objects and concentrate on the people. Some refer to them here as "the church triumphant." In Hebrews, they are referred as "the general assembly and church of the firstborn, which are written in heaven." (Hebrews 12:23) John refers to them under the image of having names "written in the book of life." He was not referring to a colossal ledger but the identity of every saved person that exists in the omniscient mind of God. The city "coming down from God out of heaven" most likely is a veiled reference to the ones already in heaven being included in the city as well as all that would be included. The symbol of bride can only refer to people. The use of "city" conveys the thought of an enormous number of people gathered as "the church of the firstborn."

If you find difficulty in relating the symbol "city" to people, we should begin with the understanding that all of the beauty of golden streets and precious jewels are only a dim picture of what heaven is really like. There is really nothing so magnificent that it can adequately represent what heaven is really like.

John has good reasons for using the city with its gates, its tremendous dimensions, and its precious metals and stones to signify great spiritual and comforting truths. I will not try to identify the significance of each item in the city. There are plenty of others who attempt that. But we are not told what was in the mind of God to convey by these symbols. They are simply beyond human comprehension. I have concluded that those who think they understand all prophecy simply don't know what they are talking about. The description of a monstrously large city was not meant to be considered literally, but figuratively. It conveyed the message that there was more than adequate room for all the saints God had been gathering throughout human history.

There are other relevant comments on the size of the city to help us understand its symbolism. The commentators have entered their opinions. People that major on the sensational are not hesitant to express their views. But when you get right down to it, a figurative understanding is the better answer. We can leave it at that. We will understand when we no longer "know in part," and view all things through "a glass darkly."

It seems that gold is the strongest item that sticks with men in the description of heaven. That may be because we treasure it, or its equivalent, the most here on earth. This gold is different; it is like clear glass. We have never seen anything like it here on earth. It is so different from the earthly gold we see. It is transparent, but still precious, and we get to walk on it, if you understand this literally. Again I will leave it to others to speculate on the meaning of the symbolic. I am content to accept it as mystical symbol, which we can truly understand when we get to heaven.

I am not going to try to identify the significance of all the precious jewels. It is clear to me that "the holy city, new Jerusalem, which comes down from God out of His heaven is a picture of all the redeemed, described as a "bride adorned for her husband." The glory of heaven to me is not a literal monstrous cube city but a place where God dwells with His people, now the "assembly of the firstborn." It is a place where God, from His throne of glory, promises to dwell with His people for eternity.

Now let us contemplate what heaven is really like. Most people hunger for some characteristic of heaven and long to be there at death. For some, the longing occurs some time before they decease. Martin Luther is reported to have said: "If you are not allowed to laugh in heaven, I don't want to go there." I do not know where laughter is spelled out as a feature of heaven, but I do know that the psalmist said that "in thy presence is fullness of joy; at thy right hand there are pleasures forevermore." (Psalm 16:11) That will be good enough for me because we will be with Him throughout the endless ages. The place simply is where God dwells and that is the best part of the description of the place.

Let us get back to our primary text: "Eye hath not seen, nor ear heard, neither entered into the heart of man, the things which God hath prepared for them that love him." (I Cor. 2:9) Better than golden streets is dwelling with God forever. To appreciate and understand this promise we can go back to the resurrection and view the body "sown in corruption; it is raised in in-corruption. It is sown in dishonor; it is raised in glory. It is sown in weakness; it is raised in power. It is sown a natural body; it is raised a spiritual body. There is a natural body and there is a spiritual body." (I Cor. 15:42-44) This is something often neglected in our thoughts, that "we shall all be changed." (I Cor. 15:52) We do not know all of what is involved in that statement, but it is obvious that we will have a whole new mode of being in the new creation. What little we do understand is that which is revealed to us in I John 3:2, "Beloved, now are we the sons of God, and it doth not yet appear what we shall be; but we know that, when he shall appear, we shall be like him; for we shall see him as he is." So that whole new mode of being may include being able to appear and disappear at will without opening doors. (John 20:19, 26) There may be human characteristics as evidenced by the fact the disciples recognized the resurrected Lord, as did over 500 witnesses. A better picture comes from the mountain of transfiguration. Evidently the disciples recognized Moses and Elijah talking with Jesus as He was transfigured before them. Then they disappeared after Jesus had allowed his disciples to get a glimpse of what it would be like as a heavenly being. Perhaps this is what Paul spoke about when he said, "But then shall I know even as I am known." (I Cor. 13:12) I take it from this statement and the other incidences that I have described that we will have no difficulty recognizing our loved ones that have preceded us. Who knows what other things, which have never entered the mind and hearts of man, that this resurrection body will experience. The secret things belong unto God.

A comprehensive feature of heaven is that we shall witness what God is doing now, and the grand show of what He will be doing throughout the endless ages. We were not here when God spoke the word and the universe came into existence, or the seven days of creation forming what he had made. We didn't see millions of his people marching through the Red Sea, in their deliverance from bondage in Egypt. We didn't see the advent of the Spirit on the day of Pentecost. We didn't see our Saviour feeding the five thousand, healing the lepers, restoring sight to the blind. However, we know the eternal, omnipotent God has great things yet to be seen as he creates a new heaven and a new earth. And from scripture, there are some affirmations we can lay hold of that give us comfort and assurance in this life. Other features of heaven are:

1. We won't be limited in our knowledge as we now are. God has given us a wonderful world book in his creation of the universe. He has given us a special revelation of himself, his plan for us, salvation by grace, rules to live by, and a glimpse of the new heavens in his word book, the Bible. All of this is to our great blessing, yet it is still true that "now we see through a glass darkly; but then face to face." Now we "know

in part," but there we shall know even as we are known. (I Cor. 13:12)

2. Jesus, Jesus, our Saviour will be there with the heavenly father and the Holy Spirit our regenerator. This is what makes it heaven - not literal golden streets.

3. We will have something to do - we will not be sitting on a cloud playing our harps. Revelation 7:15; 22:3- "Therefore are they before the throne of God, and serve him day and night in his temple: and He that sitteth on the throne will dwell with them;" " His servants shall serve him." I like work and I love God, so this appeals to me. The service described will not be wearisome toil. Service and rest will blend into one glad hymn of praise. Kipling expressed it poetically:

> When earth's last picture is painted, and the tubes are twisted and dried,
> When the oldest colors have faded, and the youngest critic has died,
> We shall rest, and, faith, we shall need it--lie down for an aeon or two,
> Till the Master of All Good Workmen shall set us to work anew!

4. Earth's trials and sorrows will be reversed. These are expressed in a series of "no mores." They are all a source of comfort and encouragement to us as we make our journey home.

5. No more sin. This is the one described by Peter: "Nevertheless we, according to his promise, look for new heavens and a new earth, wherein dwelleth righteousness." (II Peter 3:13) Sin is not a welcome experience. We struggle with it. We regret it. It causes all kinds of problems. Paul describes the "sin that dwelleth in me" and how it affected him in Romans 7:17-25. But in heaven it will be "no more."

6. No more tears (Rev. 21:4) Tear ducts apparently are unknown in the resurrection body. We have plenty of them here. This world is a veil of tears. But in heaven they will be "no more."

7. No more sorrow. We do sorrow here but not like those who have no hope. Broken relationships are hard to bear. Loss of companionship takes its toll on the human spirit. But in heaven sorrow will be "no more."

8. No more pain. Here, we may have bodily pain because this body does wear out. As soon as we are born we start marching to the grave. The older we get, the more likely our physical ailments will be the cause of pain. It just makes us long for our heavenly home. It may be emotional pain brought on by a loved one's rebellion or that pain which we share with others. It may be the pain of separation with the death of a loved one or a divorce which may mean a living death. It may be the pain of rejection by employers or broken dreams. It may be the pain of loneliness that the spouse experiences when death separates. But in heaven, pain will be "no more."

9. No more death. The apostle Paul said: "The last enemy that shall be destroyed is death." (I Cor. 15:26) We may not feel that it is an enemy when it means the release from pain and suffering in the inevitable experience of terminal illness. But we will accept the authority and description of the divine word. In heaven death will be "no more."

10. No more curse. "And there shall be no more curse." (Rev. 22:3) It is interesting that this should be singled out. Galatians 3:10-13 tells us that "Christ hath redeemed us from the curse of the law, being made a curse for us; for it is written, cursed is every one that hangeth on a tree." Calvary is over. There is only one atonement and there will never be another. The curse of the law cannot take place in heaven. All of the inhabitants are free from it and they have Christ's righteousness. There will be none to curse the saints. There will be no introduction of another Gospel. (Gal. 1:8, 9) The curse upon the serpent will be "no more" because that old serpent, the devil, is

consigned to everlasting punishment. The curse upon the ground will be over because there is a new heaven and a new earth. (cf. Genesis: Chapter 3) Whatever kind of curse exists now, in heaven, it will be "no more."

Conclusion: I am comforted by the fact that heaven is the place where God dwells with his people and that the people are symbolically portrayed as a city, the New Jerusalem, a bride, "the Lamb's wife" (Rev. 21:9), adorned by Christ's righteousness, and all are there by grace alone through faith in the Lamb of God who has taken away their sin. Where will that place be? Obviously it will be in the new heaven, the new creation, because the old has passed away. (Rev. 21:1) Both Jesus and Paul speak of a prepared and promised place for all who by faith have embraced the Christ of the cross. The assertion by Paul continues to overwhelm us: "Eye hath not seen, nor ear heard, neither have entered into the heart of man, the things God hath prepared for them that love him." (I Cor. 2:9) There is room there for you! The good news is that you can prepare for heaven now. "Believe on the Lord Jesus Christ and thou shalt be saved." (Acts 16:31)

CHAPTER 23

What is Hell Like?

Sometime ago I heard of a preacher that described the reality of hell as a place "where you would fry like a sausage for all eternity." I think the statement presumes that the resurrection body will be like the one we now have. I think the preacher can only think in terms of the literal. But to answer the question of our subject, we have to ask another question: Is it necessary to treat every description of hell literally? There are several observations I would like to make in answer to this question.

1. The only person who would know is someone who has been on the other side of the grave and come to this world with a message. That is our Lord and Saviour. Jesus used "gehenna" to describe the place of eternal punishment, which was the city dump south of Jerusalem continually burning with refuse. It was a place so full of offensiveness and hopelessness that it was a fitting symbol of the final place for all who have rejected Christ, even though it was a place prepared for the devil and his angels. Fire is frequently mentioned in connection with the message of eternal punishment.

2. Is the fire literal or a figure? One fellow minister in pondering this question, whether hell was a literal fire, could only answer, "I hope so." Before you become alarmed by that answer let me remind you that the figure is always somewhat less than the truth it vehicles. So if it is not fire it is something worse. Hell is far worse than any figure of speech, just as Christ is more than bread in a baker's shop, and more than a vine in the vineyard. So to accept fire as the ultimate description ignores other statements about hell, such as a place of "outer darkness;" a place "where their worm dieth not and the fire is not quenched" (Mark 9:43-48). Here the figure fire is associated with other figures where they are contradictory in understanding the things of earth. A "lake of fire" or "furnace of fire" could not produce great darkness. (cf Matt. 8:12; 13:42, 50; 22:13; 25:30) "Weeping and gnashing of teeth" are also characteristic of this place, and they portray symbolically great remorse. The things of eternity cannot adequately be expressed or fully understood with earthly, temporal experiences.

3. In Billy Graham's book, *A Biblical Standard for Evangelists*, an interesting and relevant observation is made on this subject: "Jesus used three words to describe hell. The first is 'darkness.' The Scripture teaches that God is light. (I John 1:5) Hell will be the opposite. Those who have rejected Christ will go into outer darkness. (Matthew 8:12) The second word He used to describe hell is 'death.' God is life. Man who is separated from the life of God and endures eternal or the second death. The third word that He used is 'fire.' Jesus used this symbol over and over. This could be literal fire, as many believe. Or it could be symbolic. God does have fires that do not burn. And also there is the figurative use of fire in the Bible. For example, in the epistle of James we read that the tongue 'is set on fire of hell.' (James 3:6) That doesn't mean that the tongue has literal combustion. I've often thought that this fire could possibly be a burning thirst for God that

is never quenched. What a terrible fire that would be – never to find satisfaction, joy, or fulfillment!"

4. To say that "fire" is not literal, but symbolic, is not to say there is no such place as hell. Hell is a real place. It is a place of separation from God forever. That is worse than a ship lost at sea without a compass; more than a child lost in a trackless wilderness or pathless forest. It is a place without Jesus and that is enough to make it a hell. We know the misery and heartache that comes from leaving Him out of our lives. It will be a hell for the lost, just to remember that they have missed the grand show of what God is doing with His saints throughout the endless ages.

5. It is a place of vile companions and despairing, disagreeable folk. There will be no fellowship there; no friendship; no song; no singing; only remorseful memories. Abraham counseled the rich man to "remember." In life he had wasted his opportunities. Now biting, bitter remorse burns within him. He remembered his five brothers and begged that they not come to that place. Our Lord describes the residents of hell as "fearful, and unbelieving, and the abominable, and murderers, and whore mongers, and idolaters, and all liars." (Revelation 21:8) A word of clarification from another passage needs to be made here. In I Corinthians 6:9-11, Paul mentions those who will not enter the kingdom of God: "Fornicators, idolaters, adulterers, thieves, drunkards, extortioners" and others. Redemption, conversion, repentance, regeneration and faith make a difference. "And such were some of you; but ye are washed, but ye are sanctified, but ye are justified in the name of the Lord Jesus, and by the Spirit of our God."

6. Hell is a place made necessary by sin and rebellion. First it was the devil and his angels. After the fall in the garden of Eden it encompasses all who will not repent and believe. The doctrine of hell is no imaginary child of darkness and superstition. All around us are the most revolting, disgusting

cesspools of sin. My sense of justice tells me if there is no hell, there ought to be one. Justice makes the doctrine of hell a necessity. The one who claims hell is unjust would not want all of the criminals turned loose on society. Every nation has its laws and its prisons. Every city has its garbage dump separating the good and useful from the spoiled, the waste, and the useless. A hell of some sort is feared almost universally by man. Even the pagan has his notion of punishment to be endured in the world beyond because of his sins. If there is no hell, then the powerful preachers of the ages have preached a colossal hoax. If there is no hell, then Christ's death on Calvary is the highest price ever paid for folly. But with the message of judgment there is also the message of grace: "For God so loved the world, that he gave his only begotten Son, that whosoever believeth in him should not perish, but have everlasting life." (John 3:16)

CHAPTER 24

What are the Believer's Crowns?

I remember as a young Christian, a Bible teacher who asserted he would receive the crowns in heaven that the Bible mentions, and "lay them at Jesus feet" as an act of heavenly worship. That is a nice thought, even a noble sentiment. I think it springs from our conscious obsession with the material. Whenever we think of crowns, we visualize some object on a person's head as a reward for achievement, honor, or the recognition of royalty. But is this the true nature of the crowns mentioned in the Bible? We shall pursue that thought as we look at the different verses of Scripture that describe the crown and the circumstances associated with them. I will try to summarize some of the wordy comments, from classical commentators, to aid us in our understanding of the true nature of the crowns.

The concept of "crowns" has its origin in the Old Testament. Of special interest is Isaiah 28:5. "In that day shall the Lord of hosts be for a crown of glory, and for a diadem of beauty, unto the residue of his people." And Isaiah 62:3: "Thou shalt also be a crown of glory in the hand of the Lord, and a royal diadem in the hand of thy God." In both of these instances the crown is a person. In the former, it is the

Lord of hosts. In the latter, it is the people of God to whom Isaiah writes. In Philippians 4:1, Paul refers to his dearly beloved brethren as "my joy and crown." In a symbolic description of the Son of God we read "on his head were many crowns." (Rev. 19:12) With this background, as we pursue the subject, I believe we can also be helped by comments from classic and respected commentators. I shall dwell on just three crowns.

THE CROWN OF RIGHTEOUSNESS

II Timothy 4:8, "Henceforth there is laid up for me a crown of righteousness, which the Lord, the righteous judge, shall give at that day; and not to me only, but also unto all them that love his appearing."

This verse describes the happiness of God's people and it is symbolized by a crown, a specific crown, "a crown of righteousness." This description agrees with the character of the saints. It is called a crown of righteousness because that perfectly describes the standing and character of that which comes from Christ's righteousness imputed to us. The crown is specified as "laid up for us." It cannot be for anybody other than the saved. It is secured for us by the promise of God. It is obtained in a righteous way. We do not obtain it by force. We do not usurp it from others. It is our own. It is a gift from the Father. We "have a legal title to it through the righteousness of Christ. Moreover, this may be expressive of the perfect holiness and righteousness of the heavenly state, and of the saints in it, wherein will dwell none but righteous persons." (Gill)

It is not material or ethereal. It was first given to us by the Father, and experienced by us. Now the result of that righteousness lasts for eterity. That may not be as simple as your conception of a material crown, but this is what the Scripture describes.

THE CROWN OF LIFE

James 1:12: "Blessed is the man that endureth temptation: for when he is tried, he shall receive the crown of life, which the Lord hath promised to them that love him."

This crown best describes the eternal happiness we have in heaven. It is an allusion to the crown of the Olympic games. It is called a crown of life because it describes something lasting. It is not something that fades away. An earthly crown often does. It is perishable, but not the life of the Christian whose existence is incorruptible. It is not merited but describes in a special way one of the bases, which was by enduring temptation. That describes all of us in some way or another, and by various degrees.

It is promised to them that love God. He has loved us with an everlasting love, and we have responded with love to Him. God who cannot lie nor deceive has promised this to us from eternity. God will never suffer His faithfulness to fail. The crown is in His hands. He has already given the crown that endures forevermore.

The crown of life is promised to all that have God's love abiding in their lives. It is for those who show that love; to the righteous sufferers who endure temptations, as well as those who worship and serve Him. It is not a debt that God owes; it rests simply on the character and promise of God.

Jamieson, Fausset and Brown sum up the whole picture in a few words: "'life' constitutes the crown, literally, *the* life, the only true life, the highest and eternal life. The crown implies a *kingdom.*" And we have been born again into that kingdom receiving the gift of eternal life.

THE CROWN OF GLORY

I Peter 5:4: "And when the chief Shepherd shall appear, ye shall receive a crown of glory that fadeth not away."

We shall try to get away from the material images that rest in our minds, and pursue the spiritual significance of the message. The nature of the crown is best described as "a garland of *victory,* the prize in the Grecian games, woven of ivy, parsley, myrtle, olive, or oak. *Our* crown is distinguished from *theirs* in that it is 'incorruptible' and 'fadeth not away,' as the leaves of theirs soon did." (*JFB*)

There is an added emphasis to this description; it "fadeth not away." The eternal glory and happiness is everlasting; it never loses its luster. It is given by the chief Shepherd to those who serve Him faithfully, which are shepherds of His flock. That is an awesome responsibility, that merits the recognition of the chief Shepherd. "Those that are found to have done their duty shall have what is infinitely better than temporal gain; they shall receive from the grand shepherd a high degree of everlasting glory, *a crown of glory that fadeth not away."* (MH)

My conclusion: I have quoted extensively from the great historical commentators to cast light on the subject before us. I have to conclude from their statements that the crowns are not something corporeal, but they are spiritual realities. I am struck by their identification with major biblical doctrines concerning the whole Christian experience. "Life" identifies with **regeneration**; the work of the Holy Spirit bringing a person "dead in trespasses and sins" into eternal life. "Righteousness" identifies with **justification**; when we are clothed with the righteousness of Christ, and stand before God justified - just as though we had never sinned. "Glory" identifies with **glorification**; the climax of our earthly experience and being made like Christ. The crown of life, the crown of righteousness, the crown of glory, the incorruptible crown are all descriptive of the whole Christian experience. They should not be viewed as material objects even though God condescends to use objects to help us understand the nature of His promises. He does this also in anthropomorphisms, using human terms and ideas to reveal the divine. Some of these terms are used in special human situations to emphasize a divine truth. For the faithful shepherd, the "crown of glory" is emphasized. For all persons going through trials, the "crown of life" is emphasized. To the Christian facing death "the crown of righteousness" is the central description. The symbol of the crown is fitting for those reigning with Christ now, (Eph. 2:5, 6) who are citizens of His kingdom, and will share in His reign throughout the endless ages. Everlasting, incorruptible, life eternal, righteousness, glory, are all apt descriptions of that free gift granted to, us not because of our own righteousness but His alone. In no case is the crown the exclusive possession of a few. Life, righteousness, and glory describe our eternal destiny. Life eternal and Christ's righteousness are ours now. The glory is reserved in heaven for us, when we are finally glorified. I am reminded again that this life is just the beginning.

CHAPTER 25

What is the Nature of the Millennium?

One of the most difficult doctrines for many to interpret in the events of the end times has to do with the nature of the Millennium. A close examination of the only Scripture where it is mentioned is Revelation 20. So let's examine the chapter carefully.

INTRODUCTION: IMPORTANCE OF THIS CHAPTER?

The first ten verses of the 20th chapter of Revelation contain the only mention in the Bible of a millennium. The period of time indicated by the meaning of the phrase, "a thousand years," is also referred to by Peter in his statement: "One day is with the Lord as a thousand years, and a thousand years as one day." (II Peter 3:8) The word millennium is not used in the Bible, but is a coined word derived from the Latin equivalent of a thousand years of time. The word has obtained the sanction of general usage because it has proved a convenient substitute for the phrase, "a thousand years."

This is the chapter that, for dispensational and premillennial theologians, suggests a theology, as it develops for them the doctrine of last things. Dr. Hamilton calls it "the very citadel of the pre-millennial system, and the norm to which all prophetic passages must be made to conform." (*The Basis of Millennial Faith,* p.126) Everything on the subject of eschatology in both the Old and New Testament must fit the framework provided by this chapter. The claim is often made to superior skills in interpretation, and the only possible Christian approach that is loyal to the Bible is by treating selected parts of this passage as literal. This a purely arbitrary claim. All others are charged with "spiritualizing" and thus robbing it of its meaning.

In light of these facts, it is important for us to properly interpret this passage before building a system of eschatology.

PRINCIPLES OF INTERPRETATION

The crux of the problem often centers in the principles of interpretation adopted by the individual interpreter. If we do not begin with valid principles of interpretation, we can end up anywhere with our conclusions.

A favorite principle of many is called "the golden rule of interpretation" which is, when the plain sense of Scripture makes common sense, seek no other sense. This is an oversimplification that is not valid. The Bible has been written in different styles with different methods of presenting its truth and must be interpreted in a way consistent with the method of presentation. There is the frequent use of metaphor, parable and figure. To interpret these literally is to miss the force of the truth for which they are a vehicle. Other important principles which should be observed for proper interpretation of a passage are: (1) The obscure passage should be interpreted in the light of the clear passage, (2) the purpose of the writer, (3) the nature of the literature, and (4) what the message meant to those who first received it. These principles cannot be ignored. This is especially true in relationship to Revelation and the passage before us. We accept this as code language. It is an apocalyptic writing. There is a certain amount of obscurity about such literature. One of

155

its prominent features is the use of "vision" as a literary device by which writers introduce their conceptions. This literature was written in dangerous times. The personal safety of both writer and reader was endangered if their persecutors understood the true meaning of the book. Like parables, it was intended both to reveal and to conceal the truth. The purpose of the writer was not to cover up his message, but to make it increasingly vivid by "unveiling" through signs and symbols. The Christians could understand—the persecutors would not. Symbolism is a system in which qualities, ideas, principles, etc., are represented by things concrete. They are used for the expression of spiritual ideas. *The literal truth lies in what is symbolized.* The action or truth is what is literal. The symbol means what the action intends it to mean where the writer uses it. He adapts the symbol to suit his message. Our task is to discern what is a symbol and then what that symbol means.

George Fletcher makes a good point when he says: "While we should carefully shun all spiritualization, however ingenious, which robs the Word of God of its true force and beauty, we should shun with equal care a false literalism which extracts error out of figurative statements." (The Millennium, p. 14)

A close and fair examination of this passage, I believe, will show how absurd and unreasonable the conclusions of the literalist, even if their own principles of interpretation are applied. The truth is "the plain sense" of this Scripture does not "make common sense" when treated as literal rather than symbolic, which we will proceed to illustrate and explain in section III.

The only logical alternative to the dispensational and premillennial systems is what is commonly known as amillennialism. This common label is a misnomer. Amillennialism means "no millennium." No amillennialist that I know holds to this position. The question concerns the "nature" of the millennium, not the "fact." The great question is not "when" but "where"—in what realm do the described events take place? Are they in the realm of the natural, or in the spiritual?

The great sin of the amillennialist is supposed to be that of "spiritualizing" the passage rather than taking it literally— in spite of the fact that the teaching corresponds perfectly with the teachings of Jesus and Paul. My concern is, the great mistake of all varieties of the pre-millennial system is to arbitrarily assert that "a thousand years" has to be taken literally in a passage and a book which is manifestly symbolic. A close study of the use of symbolism in this passage will bear that out.

STATEMENT OF CONTENT

Before looking closely at the symbolism of this passage, a brief statement of content is in order. There are three scenes in the drama of this chapter that concern us. The first one occurs on earth, verses 1-3. The second transpires in heaven, verses 5-6, and reveals things that are taking place in the spiritual realm. Look at it carefully for the "plain sense," if you will. The location is in heaven, not on earth. It is concerned with spiritual realities, not physical supervision of a material kingdom. The "literal" action is in the present, not the future. The third scene returns to earth, verses 7-10, and continues the history of Satan, which is the main theme of this passage, not the millennium.

There is not a word or hint this passage describes a literal thousand year period during which Christ would reign in bodily presence on this earth, from a Palestinian kingdom, with the capital at Jerusalem. Nothing said here indicates that the people of God in their resurrection bodies will share in this reign upon the earth over a political kingdom. Nothing here indicates that the Jews will be restored to their ancient territory and invested with world supremacy. Any injection of these ideas into this passage must come from those who want to make it fit their theological system through the careful connection of "proof-texts." This is the launching pad for the rockets of speculation. If a literal thousand year reign by Christ is not found here, then a re-examination of other prophetic scriptures is in order. Since there is no other place in the New Testament to develop a doctrine of a

Palestinian millennial kingdom, it requires a re-evaluation of the Old Testament prophecies of a golden age and their relationship to the spiritual kingdom and eternal kingdom mentioned so frequently in the New Testament message. That will be difficult for some people, and so the premises I have stated will be rejected. I realize this is an extensive study that requires its own careful comparison of Scripture with Scripture and cannot concern us at this point in determining the actual message of Revelation 20:1-10.

In summary, let me emphasize that a close examination of this passage nowhere indicates that the reign is to be at a future time upon the earth. The scene is in heaven of the martyred saints reigning with Christ and describes an experience they share with others called "the first resurrection." The passage is full of symbolism, which is consistent with John's method and purpose in writing. A consistent literalism would limit the participants of this reign to those who "were beheaded for the witness of Jesus, and for the word of God, and which had not worshiped the beast, neither his image, neither had received his mark upon their foreheads, or in their hands." (v.4) This description literally does not describe all the saints of all ages.

USE OF SYMBOLISM

To understand the message of this passage close attention must be given to each symbol. Some are easier to identify than others, but the passage is rich in symbolism, and to understand their meaning is a giant step toward receiving the spiritual message of the passage.

1. "An angel." I believe Phillip Mauro is right when he says:

> The evidence warrants the conclusion that the 'angel' who bound the Devil is none other than Christ Himself. None of the angelic hosts is great enough to bind Satan (Jude v. 9). To the angel who opens the bottomless pit (chapter 9:1, 2) the key was given; but this 'Angel' has the key thereof; and for the interpretation of this statement we may properly refer to the

declaration of the Lord in Chapter 1:18, that He has 'the keys of hell (hades) and of death.' (*Of Things Which Must Shortly Come to Pass,* p. 583)

If your literal interpretation prevents you from identifying Jesus with the angel, I can only remind you that Jesus is revealed as the "angel of the Lord" in the Old Testament. He is also the greater "strong man" of Mark 3:27. "Let me illustrate this further. Who is powerful enough to enter the house of a strong man like Satan and plunder his goods? Only someone even stronger--someone who could tie him up and then plunder his house." (*New Living Translation*)

2. "Key." The key obviously represents something spiritual, for the abyss could not be opened with a physical key. The fact that we identify this as spiritual does not make it less real than something in the physical. It is more real. (cf. II Cor. 3:18) The key kept in heaven simply suggests that Christ has jurisdiction over Satan, and it is one of the four symbols to portray Satan's limitations and the guarantee of the security of his limitations. The other symbols are the chain, the pit, and the seal.

3. "The bottomless pit" or the abyss. A vivid literalism visualizes the place of Satan's abode as some sort of hole in the ground, somewhere on this earth, where an ancient serpent is bound by a real metal chain and a door or lid of some sort secures the entrance. The symbolism of "the dragon, that old serpent" is explained by a brief identification. It is "Satan," the Hebrew name meaning "opposer or adversary" and "the Devil," a Greek word meaning "false accuser," "slanderer." And what is the symbolism of the abyss? It is simply a representation of a state in which the descent and departure from God shall be endless but is not the final destination. The place for binding is not the same as the final doom. This is his present place of abode from which he carries on his activities. A contemporary comparison would be the county jail where accused prisoners are detained prior to their sentencing and the state penitentiary to which they are assigned for the final punishment. The abyss is a temporary abode, the lake of fire is the eternal abode.

4. "A great chain." Surely no one can conceive of this as a physical object because Satan, as a spiritual being, cannot be bound with an iron chain. The chain is simply linked with other symbols to demonstrate the sovereign authority of Christ over Satan. Peter tells us that the angels who sinned, which includes Satan, have been delivered "into chains of darkness, to be reserved unto judgment." (II Peter 2:4.) This has already happened and yet Peter says: "Be sober, be vigilant, because your adversary, the Devil, as a roaring lion, walketh about, seeking whom he may devour." (I Peter 5:8) Obviously he is a chained lion and can go only as far as the chain allows. So the chain in Revelation 20 represents a restraint and restriction of movement, privilege, and power laid upon the Devil by one possessed of superior power. The restriction is spelled out here, "that he should deceive the nations no more." No other effect on human life is mentioned.

5. "Seal." The "seal" is also better interpreted from New Testament usage than by trying to make it a literal material entity. The Ephesian believers are said to be sealed by the Holy Spirit, which simply means they were appointed to a certain destiny. (Eph. 4:30, 1:13) The sealing was the guarantee of a certain destination. I believe that the sealing of Satan has the same significance in this passage. The doom of Satan was sealed by our Lord's death on the cross.

6. "Thrones." The vision continues of countless "thrones" occupied by men from earth in their disembodied state as "souls." The locality is obviously heaven whereas verses 1-3 are on earth. The picture of the ones occupying the "thrones" does not fit living Jews or Christians each having a throne in Jerusalem or anywhere else on earth. The occupied thrones were simply symbolic of the participation of the saints in Christ's continual victories.

7. "The first resurrection." The biggest question of literalism versus symbolism concerns the identity of "the first resurrection." Does Revelation 20 anywhere indicate that it is a bodily resurrection from the grave? An identifying statement is made: "This is the first resurrection." (v.5) To what do these words refer? What is the antecedent of "this?" What does "this" describe? All that is described in 20:4, sitting upon "throne" and exercising "judgment"—living and

reigning with Christ a thousand years. Obviously, "the second death" does not mean bodily death, and a close examination of the passage makes it clear that the "first resurrection" does not mean bodily resurrection. It is a metaphorical use of the word. If this is hard to accept, it should not be. The saying of one thing and the meaning of another is common in Revelation. It is a distinctive characteristic of the Revelation, since John chose to write in the language of figures, signs, and symbols. The prophets commonly employed figurative language, as did Jesus. For example, when Christ took bread and said, "this is my body," only those who understand Him "literally" come up with the heresy of transubstantiation.

It is the rule, rather than the exception, for John to employ such usage in his book. When he speaks of the "key of David" in 3:7, he means the power of David. And when he speaks of "David" here, it is obviously not "David," but David's descendant, Jesus, the Son of God. The robes of the saints are not actual robes, but souls, hearts, lives.

The robes are "made white in the blood of the lamb." Actual blood does not make garments white. The giving of Christ's life ("the life of the flesh is in the blood") is what avails for the cleansing. The Lamb is not an animal, but Jesus.

It is clear that when John speaks of death, he is speaking of it in the spiritual sense. He does not mean that the "lake of fire" is itself "the second death," but that it signifies the eternal punishment, separation, banishment to which the unbelieving belong. He doesn't choose to make physical death the first death, but included it in the banishment and punishment that came upon the race as a result of the first sin. It is no new thing for the Bible to speak of death in the spiritual sense. (See John 5:24, John 8:51, John 11:25-26, Romans 5:14, Romans 6:9, Romans 8:6, Ephesians 2:1.) In fact, in the New Testament, the unconverted are always regarded as existing in a state of death and servitude to sin. Death is not the extinction of man's life, but it is a state of being, spiritually speaking.

It is just as clear that John and the New Testament writers do not always mean bodily resurrection when they speak of the resurrection.

At conversion, man's natural condition of spiritual death is reversed—and he lives and reigns. First, he passes from death into life. Instead of being under the authority of sin, he shares the authority of Christ; he reigns with Him. This living and reigning are in the spiritual sphere, not the natural. Our life is not here; it is fixed with Christ in God. (Col.3:3) We are not seated on thrones in the physical sense in this life, but just as we live with and in a risen Lord in the heavenlies, so likewise do we reign with Him here and now.

The writer of the Apocalypse shows, by what he has written in his Gospel, what he learned from his Lord, of a "resurrection" which preceded the resurrection of the body. Why should it seem strange then that he would call it "the first resurrection?" In John 5:24, Jesus said that "He that heareth my word, and believeth on Him that sent me, hath everlasting life, and shall not come into condemnation; but is passed from death unto life." Having eternal life and passing into life is equivalent to "they lived" – passing out of death is equivalent to "over these the second death hath no authority."

Again, in John 11:25-26, Jesus says "I am the resurrection and the life; he that believeth in me though he were dead yet shall he live; and whomsoever liveth and believeth in me shall never die." Phillip Mauro is right when he contends, "Here is a 'resurrection' which is wholly apart from that of the body; and one that comes before that of the body." (*The Hope of Israel: What is It?*, p. 251) And Jesus' statement, that "He that liveth and believeth in me shall never die" is equivalent again to the words "they lived...over these the second death has no authority."

If this is not enough evidence, note the equally strong confirmations in the writings of Paul, who refers time and again to a resurrection which is the experience of those who have not yet experienced bodily death and resurrection. (Eph. 2:56; Col. 2:12; Col. 3:1; Romans 6:13) He describes believers who have not died physically as "risen with Christ" and "alive from the dead." He also supports John's description of reigning saints. We are even now sitting together in the heavenlies with Christ. (Eph. 1:19-22, 2:4-6)

So these common conceptions in the New Testament, of Christians sitting on thrones and reigning as Christ does, are not something that is yet to be. This has been going on since the death and exaltation of Christ. So says John in the language of mystic symbolism which he employs throughout the Apocalypse. Unsaved people are spiritually dead—the Christian life is a spiritual resurrection.

9. "The binding of Satan." This action is symbolic and is better interpreted by clear statements in the Gospels than by trying to force an extreme liberalism into the picture. Jesus said, "How can one enter into a strong man's house, and spoil his goods, except he first bind the strong man? And then he will spoil his house." (Matthew 12:28-29) Jesus was making it plain in figurative language that Satan does not willingly surrender his subjects. "When he is rendered powerless to retain his prey and made powerless to recapture his escaped captives, the explanation is that he is bound." (George Murray, *Millennial Studies*) This is a description of a spiritual reality that is consistent with what Jesus did. That is exactly what happened through the work of Christ and became a reality through faith in Christ. Believers have been delivered from the power of darkness. (Col. 1:13) Also the writer to the Hebrews emphasizes that the Son of God became man in order that "through death He might destroy him that had the power of death, that is, the Devil." Hebrews 2:14, 15 and Colossians 2:14, 15 make it clear that, by His cross, Christ despoiled principalities and powers, openly triumphing over them. This is the binding of the "strong man." This is the binding of Satan in Revelation 20:2.

Furthermore, if anyone finds it difficult to accept this as a "binding" in light of Satan's activity today, it is still consistent with the imprisonment of Satan and his restricted activity described by Peter, as well as the extent and purpose of the binding described by John which was the inability to deceive the nations.

10. "A thousand Years." So far it is obvious, I have not taken literally many of the symbols used to communicate this message to the early Christians. The angel, chain, bottomless pit, seal, binding, first resurrection, second death, thrones, etc. Neither the actual wording nor enlightenment of New Testament teachings require it or

justify it. So then, why inject arbitrarily into the passage the treating of 1000 years as a literal period of time?

Why the figure of 1000 years? God, who inhabits eternity, is not affected by the passage of time as we are but is independent of all time limitations. This is clear from II Peter 3:8, "One day is with the Lord as a thousand years, and a thousand years as one day." The indefinite period of time is totally consistent with the message of the Gospels that "no man knoweth the time" when Jesus will return. While the events of Revelation 20:5-6 are taking place in heaven, they are not limited by calendar years. The time is only limited by the eternal purpose and sovereign will of God. When this full period of time has run its course in the plan of God, the next event will take place—the loosing of Satan and the final judgment.

The figure 1000 is a perfect vehicle to convey this spiritual truth. The only other place the term is used in the Bible, it denotes an indefinite period of time— time as men regard time does not apply to God. In terms of ancient numerology used throughout Revelation, "ten" is a number of completeness. Thousand is a heightened multiple of "ten." So it conveys a strong figure of completeness for an indefinite and possibly a long period of time.

What is the period of time covered by the symbol of a thousand years? It is clearly the time when Satan is unable to "deceive the nations." I take that to be the period between the death of Christ to a short time before the consummation of the age, when Satan is "loosed for a little season." It is this time that the Gospel is preached and God is gathering a redeemed people.

The assertion that the number 1000 has to be taken literally, it appears to me, is purely arbitrary. I say that in light of the obvious and abundant symbolism of the chapter as already reviewed. I do not think it unreasonable, but only natural in light of the fact that numbers throughout the book of Revelation are symbolic in keeping with the apocalyptic nature of the book. The promise to the church at Smyrna was they would have tribulation "ten days." (Rev. 2:10) I see no reason to take that with mathematical exactness, but as an indefinite measure of time. In Chapter 9:5, 10, some were to be "tormented five months." Five is the number of incompleteness, an indication of a plague of considerable length, though great and prolonged, was not complete and final. The 144,000 is clearly a symbolic number representing the whole company of the saved. Twelve times twelve is the signature of the eternal city, the home of all the redeemed. This multiple of twelve coupled with the multiple of ten is used to express symbolically the complete number of the saints, not a literal count. Every place a number is used in this apocalyptic literature it needs to be carefully examined to discern the spiritual message.

So to understand the purposeful use of 1000, let us go back to the symbolism of numbers. Ten stands for a rounded total and is one of the complete numbers. A thousand is the cube of 10, and so symbolizes the vastness of number of time. It is used in other places in this way, and so it it is reasonable and logical to follow that interpretation here. In Psalm 50:10, we are told "the cattle upon a thousand hills" belong to the Lord. I do not take this to be a literal 1000 hills, but to indicate that the total amount of all the cattle on all the hills of the world are His. Notice the same sense in Psalm 84:10, "For a day in thy courts is better than a thousand," and Psalm 90:4, "For a thousand years in thy sight are but as yesterday;" and Psalm 91:7, "A thousand shall fall at thy side, and ten thousand at thy right hand..."

So the 1000 years represent a complete period of time, indefinite to us, but definite to God. He alone knows the actual years. It is the period during which the souls of the departed saints reign with Christ. It is the cycle of time which extends from our Lord's first advent to His second advent. It includes the binding and loosing of Satan. In general, it represents the whole Christian era. I see no need to pinpoint its beginning at the incarnation, the crucifixion, the resurrection, or the ascension and ending with the "loosing" or the return. The saints do not cease to reign with the "loosing" of Satan. Heerboth sums it up well in his statement: "Then these 'thousand years' together with 'the little season' during which Satan is loosed again, constitute the time of the New Testament, beginning with Christ's redemption, and lasting to Judgment Day. For immediately after Satan's last assault upon the beloved city, the Christian Church,

God's judgment will follow (vs. 9-15). (*The Millennium and the Bible,* p. 34)

11. "Gog and Magog." These were the last great enemies that Israel faced in the inter-biblical period and so they "serve well as symbols for the barbarous people who rally with the devil about the camp of the saints." (Ray Summers, W*orthy is The Lamb,* p. 207) No theological system with which I am familiar treats these literally although they may prefer to do so. The literal identity of these names in Ezekiel is this: "Gog is a name for Antiochus Epiphanes and Magog a name for the nation over which he was prince." (Summers, p. 206) Many premillennialists who insist Ezekiel and John were writing about the same future event will equate Gog and Magog with the northern European powers, headed up by Russia. (See Scofield Bible, Footnote on Ezekiel 38, p. 383, for an example.) But that is not the literal Gog and Magog of Ezekiel or Revelation, and so they have made it symbolism.

It is quite evident from comparing Ezekiel and Revelation, the two prophecies are not literally identical as George Fletcher appropriately points out :

> The Gog of Ezekiel comes down from the 'North' parts upon Palestine, while the Gog of Revelation comes up from the 'four corners of the earth.' In Ezekiel, he is spoken of as coming 'against the returned exiles' from Babylon (38:11, 14), whereas in Revelation he comes against 'the camp of the saints and beloved city' (a symbolic expression of the New Testament Churches) or people of God. The sixth part of the armies of Ezekiel's Gog escape destruction (39:2) while in Revelation 20 Gog and his forces are 'devoured' by fire sent down from heaven. From this evidence, we conclude that Ezekiel and the apostle John were not writing of the same events." (*The Millennium,* p.31)

The greatest difficulty with pre-millennial assumptions is their position that this great battle takes place at the close of their kind of millennium, but in Ezekiel 39:1ff, the destruction of Gog and Magog comes before the bringing back of "the captivity of Jacob," which pre-millennialists say is the beginning of their millennium.

So the question is really, what do the terms Gog and Magog symbolize? Contemporary world powers of a future date or a spiritual enemy over which Christ and the people will triumph? I agree with Fletcher: "Here the expressions symbolize the hosts of infidelity in a revived Paganism arrayed against the truth of God for a 'little season' before the Second Advent." (p.72) Actually, the symbol was very appropriate to typify the last great death-struggle between Paganism and Historic Christianity. Fletcher explains why :

> The armies of Gog and Magog were very numerous, and therefore, adequately symbolize the world-wide universal opposition to the people of God in the <u>end of the Christian era</u>. The tribulation under Antiochus Epiphanes, though very severe, was nevertheless, of very brief duration; hence, it foreshadows the brief final tribulation which will occur at the close of our present dispensation. The armies of Syria met an unexpected and complete defeat; likewise, its antitype—a godless world arrayed against the church—comes to a sudden end. Just as Antiochus, the Illustrious, tried to stamp out the Mosaic worship, so will Satan in the last great conflict between truth and error, endeavor to stamp out Christian worship. (p.33)

Heerboth also agrees: "'Gog and Magog' are evidently, as in Ezekiel 38 and 39, symbolical names or terms for all powers 'in the four quarters of the earth,' they are enemies of the true Church of the living God." (*The Millennium and The Bible,* p.33)

I have selected only ten items from this passage to demonstrate the thorough and consistent symbolism of the passage. There are many more. To insist on literalism would require the "beast" be an animal, not a man or civil power. The book of life is not a colossal ledger but a record kept in the omniscient mind of God. Clearly the events described are in the spiritual realm. The two actors in the first scene are spiritual beings. The "key," "great chain," "seal," and "thrones" are spiritual, not material. The "abyss" is a spiritual locality. The binding and sealing of Satan are spiritual actions. Then why all the fear of "spiritualizing" when the symbols are intended to convey spiritual truth?

Obviously, it makes better sense to interpret the symbols in light of other biblical truths. What we have throughout this book are spiritual realities described in human terminology. The human is always inadequate to fully represent the divine. But if we do not accept the symbolic intent of the human we will never discover even partially the divine message of the symbol.

I would rather be charged with "spiritualizing" where the evidence demands it than be guilty of "carnalizing" when there is no justification for it.

SUMMARY OF MESSAGE.

There is not a hint in this passage to warrant the idea that the 1000 years is a literal period of time during which Christ would reign in bodily presence over the world and with Him the people of God in their resurrected bodies. The only contribution of this passage to dispensational and pre-millennial systems is the name "millennium."

We have demonstrated clearly the symbolic nature of things and actions mentioned in this passage. If we are guilty of "spiritualizing" in applying the same technique to "1000 years," then so be it. To me, the text and the context both demand it. The more I study the passage, the more evident it is to me that the demand to treat the 1000 years as a literal period of time is purely arbitrary but necessary to support a preconceived millennial system.

As with all of the sacred writings, we contend that they must have had meaning to those who first received them. This is true of

Revelation and of this passage in chapter 20. They have passed the first death and the second death (eternal separation from God) has no jurisdiction over them.

What John says of the deceased believers is also true of the living saints. The Kingdom of God includes all of the redeemed, both in heaven and on earth. But it is the heavenly phase of the kingdom which John portrays symbolically. This fit John's purpose in writing. To those who read or heard him, they got the message, and it gave them courage to die for the name of Jesus. They had the assurance that while their bodies slumbered in the dust, their souls would reign with Christ. As with all the Scriptures, there is a message for every age as well. Ray Summers has given a good statement in the following summary:

> Revelation is a series of apocalyptic images given for the assurance of the people of God that Christ is going to be victorious over all opposition. For the Christians of John's day the assurance was given by showing the victory of Christ over the system of emperor worship because that was the greatest enemy of Christ in that day. The same assurance is given to Christians in every age. Find the greatest enemy of Christ (whether corrupt religion, godless government, social anarchy, or any other), put it in the place of emperor worship, and see its eventual failure as the living Christ, the redeeming Lamb, marches to victory over chaotic world conditions—Worthy is the Lamb." (*Worthy is The Lamb,* p. 208)

CONCLUSION

I believe you can readily see the difficulty of arriving at truth from these chapters. There are many more, which I have not covered, but I considered these outstanding. To carefully examine what others have taught concerning biblical beliefs is not to deny the Christian faith or to question Christian orthodoxy. It is the responsibility of every one of us to keep our minds open to further illumination from the Scriptures. When we do that, we discover that some of our conclusions are too simple, or just plain erroneous. It is then that we can rejoice in truth.

In our day, the task of discernment is more difficult. For example, when we hear a favorite preacher, we are tempted to embrace everything he teaches. We are never encouraged to check it out. It is so much easier just to accept it as true. It is just as possible with the Holy Spirit's help to be discerning and arrive at truth. At the same time we can receive blessing from other truths proclaimed and established through study. The difficulty is further evident when there is so much proclaimed as truth which is only partially true. Yet the proclaimers are so popular. I would especially note the prosperity gospel preachers that dominate Christian television. It is when we are willing to deal with the controversial, which is always difficult, that we are able to continue learning.

Bible Translations:
ASV *American Standard Version*
CEV *Contemporary English Version*
ESV *English Standard Version*
HCSB *Holcomb Christian Standard Bible*
ISV *International Standard Version*
KJV *King James Version*
LITV *Literal Translation of the Holy Bible*
NLT *New Living Translation*
RV *Revised Version*
MSG The Message
YLT *Young's Literal Translation*

Bible Commentaries:
Albert Barnes' Notes on the Whole Bible
JFB Jamieson, Faucet, Brown, *Commentary Critical and Explanatory on the Whole Bible*
John Gill's Exposition of the Entire Bible
John Wesley's Notes on the Bible
KJV Bible Commentary
Matthew Henry's Commentary on the Whole Bible
Matthew Henry's Concise Commentary
Robertson's Word Pictures in the New Testament
With The Word Commentary

Websites:

Catholic.org
Concordia Lutheran Conference
Geocities, Rain Forest 4620 population
Global Warming.org
Jesus is Saviour website
Reformed.org
Wikepedia

Authors:

Bullock, Miles, *What Christians Believe*, 1879, Twos W. Dunton & Co.

Cole, C.D., 1944, *Definitions of Doctrine*, Providence Baptist Ministries

Environmental Stewardship in the Judea-Christian Tradition, Acton Institute

Fletcher, George B., 1947, *The Millennium*, Bible Truth Depot

Graham, Billy, 1984, *A Biblical Standard for Evangelists*, Worldwide Publications

Greene, Oliver B., 1970, *Bible Prophecy*, The Gospel Hour, Inc.

Hamilton, Floyd E., 1942, *The Basis of Millennial Faith*, Wm. B. Eerdmans Publishing Co.

Heerboth, L. A., 1947, *The Millennium and the Bible*, Bible Truth Depot

Hiscox, Edward Thurston, 1894, *The New Directory for Baptist Churches*

Hobbs, Herschel, 1954, *Studies in Hebrews*, Sunday School Board

Kennedy, D. James, 2005, *Skeptics Answered*, Multnomah Books

Klaus, Vaclav, 2007, *Blue Planet in Green Shackles*, Competitive Enterprise Institute

Ladd, George Eldon, 1978, *The Last Things*, Wm. B. Eerdmans Publishing Co.

Mauro, Philip, T., 1929, *The Hope of Israel: What Is It?*, Hamilton Bros.

Mauro, Philip, *Of Things Which Soon Must Come to Pass*, 1933, The Colonial Press, Inc.

Moore, Thomas Gale, 1998, *Climate of Fear*, Cato Institute

Murray, George L., 1951, *Millennial Studies*, Bible Truth Depot

Robertson, A.T., 1933, *Word Pictures in the New Testament*, Broadman Press

Strong, Augustus Hopkins, 1909, *Systematic Theology*, The Griffith and Rowland Press

Summers, Ray, 1951, *Worthy is the Lamb*, Broadman Press

ACKNOWLEGEMENTS

Special thanks are extended to my family
for their steadfast assistance
in the necessary editing services here at home.
I am fortunate to have two children, who
have had some theological training,
and advanced education to assist me.
I want to thank the staff at CrossBooks for their
patience, understanding, and guidance
through the completion of this project. I am
especially indebted to Kayla Stobaugh,
the coordinator at Crossbooks Publishing.

Printed in the United States
By Bookmasters